ROBERT IVINS was born in 1956, the son of a Nottingham university professor of agriculture, on a large working farm. From the age of five he spent all his spare time in the farm workshop as the apprentice's apprentice, mending tractors and a 1948 Land Rover.

Learning to drive at seven, in a 1935 Austin 7 Ruby which he still owns, he attended grammar school and college before joining a specialist Land Rover concern. A short time later, he set up his own garage before moving to a farm in the Staffordshire moorlands in 1987 to start a specialist Land Rover business.

Robert has owned many Land Rovers since passing his driving test at 17. He has a growing collection of historic and prototype Land Rovers and is proudest of RO8 which he found and restored to original condition. Today, pre-production Land Rover number 8 is the oldest Land Rover licenced for use on the public roads.

Know Your Land Rover is published by:
LRO Books Ltd.,
The Hollies,
Botesdale,
Diss, Norfolk IP22 1BZ
© LRO Books Ltd 1991

Fuel

MANY Land Rover and Range Rover owners seem to be very conscientious people who want to do their bit to reduce global environmental pollution by the use of lead free fuel. As an added bonus, there is a tax differential which makes lead free petrol some 10p per gallon cheaper in the UK. Diesel, incidentally, is entirely lead free.

ALL V8 engines 1970 to date will run on lead free ALL the time with no modifications at all except post 1981 high compression and EFi engines which need the timing retarding 3°.

ALL 90/110 2.5 petrol engines will run with no adjustment on lead free.

NO 2.25 engine i.e. Series II, III and 110 up to 1984 will run on lead free UNLESS the complete cylinder head or hard exhaust valve seats from the 2.5 engines are fitted.

NO 2.6, 2.0 or 1.6 engine will run on lead free fuel.

The effect of using lead free in an engine not designed for it is not instant. It will not "conk out" just down the road from the filling station but will suffer gradual and PERMANENT damage to the valve gear. It will cost more to repair the burnt valve seats and valves than the saving on fuel.

Older V8 engines which have not run before on lead free will not be harmed at all providing normal servicing is carried out.

What is lead in petrol?
The lead in petrol is a compound called Tetra Etheyl Lead, which is added as an octane improver to boost available power in an engine. It was developed in WW2 for aircraft use and has been used since in car fuel.

What happens if I use unleaded in my engine?
If you use unleaded in an engine not designed for it then premature failure of the exhaust valve seats will result. This is due to the higher burning temperature of the lead free fuel. If the engine has exhaust valve seats of suitable material, as fitted in Rover V8 and 2.5 litre petrol engines, then this will not happen.

Fuel additives — any good?

If I use unleaded will my engine be less powerful?
Yes, but you will probably only notice at past the legal maximum speed limit.

Will my vehicle run on unleaded?
No, if it is a 2.25 litre engine unless you change the cylinder head for a 2.5 or have the old head bored out and 2.5 litre valve seats fitted (ETC 6278). No, if it is an "F" head engine — 1.5 litre, 2.0 litre and 2.6 litre. Yes, if it is a 2.5 litre (Ninety and One Ten). Yes, if it is a V8 (Range Rover, 109, Ninety, One Ten).

Will I have to make any adjustments?
No, if you have a 2.5 engine. No, if you have a V8 low compression Range Rover (all Ninety/One Ten and Range Rover up to 1981 and some Range Rover post 1981). Yes, if you have a high compression Range Rover (Compression ratio 9.35.1) or UK specification EFi. All that is required is simply to retard the ignition timing by 3 degrees (are you sure that your ignition timing is spot on, anyway — try unleaded and if the engine doesn't "pink", you're OK, but have the ignition properly set at the next service).

Can I run my Series One on lead free?
The official factory view is that you *cannot*, but as the vehicles have been out of production for thirty years, testing by the factory has not been carried out. The engines do have exhaust valve seats of a harder material that the block's cast iron, unlike the later 2.25 litres engines. Also, the engines originally ran on "Pool" petrol which was not of the best quality. My *personal* view is that they will run on lead free if the valve gear and engine are in *perfect* condition before using unleaded petrol. If the valves are a bit pitted and have poor seats then they will quickly burn out. The risk is up to you.

How much will it cost to convert?
If you have a 2.5 or V8 the cost is nothing, or a small fee to have the ignition retimed (free if included with a routine service).

If you have a 2.25 the cost of a new 2.5 head is not economically viable, so the alternative is to have the head machined to take the 2.5 inserts (ETC 6278) at £6.58 each plus VAT and probably £50 to £75 to have the head reconditioned at the same time. If the job is done DIY, the cost will probably be £150-£200 including gaskets, antifreeze, etc.

There would probably be an improvement in mpg with a top end overhaul, but at the present price differential of 10p and 18 miles per gallon, the investment of £200 would not show a return until 36,000 miles had been travelled. So, unless you are very ecology conscious, or the price differential increases dramatically or 2 star becomes unavailable, then it does not make sense to convert a 2.25 to run on lead free.

If, however, you are reconditioning an engine anyway, the fitting of the valve seats will only increase your expense marginally so the return will probably be after only 5,000 miles.

I have read in LRO of the benefit of using Carbonflo in petrol engines. I own a Ninety with normally aspirated 2.5 diesel engine. Can I use Carbonflo in this engine and would it have the same benefits such as lower fuel consumption?
It is possible to use in a diesel engine, but the main purpose is to make it possible to use unleaded petrol in a vehicle which cannot normally use it. As the use of Carbonflo has not been totally proved yet, I suggest not using it in your diesel. Recent tests by Rover have shown that, on the four cylinder car engines not designed to run lead free, valve seat regression still occurs when using Carbonflo and lead free

fuel. Time will tell with Land Rover two and a quarter engines if they are protected with the use of Carbonflo.

Eighteen months ago I took early retirement. The first thing I did was to refurbish my 1973 vehicle, of course I have kept it in good order.
The original engine I have kept as a spare and would like to convert it to run on unleaded petrol, could you please inform me where to get drawings or information on conversion.
Any engine machining company should be able to bore out your head and press in the valve seat inserts (ETC 6278) and recut them. Also have the inlet valve seats recut at the same time.

I have been using unleaded petrol in my Ninety 2.5 litre. However, at a recent service I found signs of burning on the spark plugs and I have reverted to leaded. Advice please.
Your 90 2.5 petrol will run perfectly on lead free petrol with no alteration. The burnt plugs are more likely caused by using poor quality plugs or the timing or mixture wrongly set, or simply too many miles since they were last replaced.
Keep on using lead free if the engine is not set properly after its recent service.

Recently we have had trouble with the engine misfiring and stalling, even when hot. On our list of possible causes to check was a leak on the air intake to the carburettor (one of our first priorities, as the vacuum guage was reading very low). Having located the air intake manifold we noticed a significant difference between the diagrams in the manuals and our engine. On the air intake manifold is a small pipe which in the manuals was fitted with a blank plug — ours had a hose attached. This we traced to a cylindrical metal box (about 2' long and about 8" in diameter) located under the nearside front wheelarch. Also attached to this box were the vacuum guage and a third pipe which led to what appeared to be a servo for the brake(?!).
We have been unable to discover what all this apparatus is for and wondered if you might be able to shed some light on the matter? By the way, the 'box' had a had a hole in it; disconnecting it from the air intake manifold and replacing it with a blank plug seems to have solved our original problem with no immediately apparent side-effects.
However, it appears that 2 star petrol is now unavailable in our area, so we have been using 4 star in its place. Is this likely to have any adverse effect on the engine?
I would be grateful if you could help with another problem we have experienced: Our manual states that the type of spark plugs that should be used, depends upon the compression ratio of the engine. We have a 1974, Series III 88 Land Rover (2¼ litre petrol) and apparently it is possible to have a C/R of either 7:1 or 8:1. How would we be able to tell which we have?
Most of the 7:1 compression engines were fitted to export models but without quoting engine no. I cannot tell you which type you have fitted to your Land Rover. I would guess that it is an 8:1.
The tank under the wing is a vacuum reservoir for the brake system. It is not a standard fitting for your model. It is

A smell of petrol

commonly fitted to vehicles used for towing a large trailer fitted with vacuum brakes.

If the reservoir is holed then the remote brake servo will not be working and needs removing Renew the brake pipe between the master cylinder and the multi way union mounted on the chassis at the back of the engine bay on the o/s just below the steering box and bleed the system with new brake fluid.

I previously replaced the old Solex with a new Weber carb on my Series II, 2.25 lump. Since then I have replaced the old leaky fuel pump which has given me a perplexing problem. When the engine is hot and if I stop the engine for up to half an hour I get a smell of petrol in the cab and upon setting off again I experience severe fuel starvation causing the engine to stop unless travelling fast on an open road.

Either you have a faulty fuel pump which allows fuel to bleed back in to the tank or the petrol pipe is routed too close to sources of heat which is causing vapour locking in the pipe. I would guess it is faulty. Get an overhaul kit for your old pump then replace it in the vehicle.

I own an ex-MOD, Series IIA which, because of army alternations has its petrol tanks under the driver's and front passenger's seats. The front and rear of a Land Rover are well protected from collision damage, but the sides only have the outriggers for defence. The driver is fairly safe, because of the height of the seat, but the petrol tanks appear to be exposed to damage. The outriggers only provide limited protection and the aluminium 'trim' gives none. A car hitting the side of the Land Rover would probably crush the fuel tank and spill petrol, creating an explosion risk. I am in the process of fitting scaffolding runner boards to offer some protection, but it is still a concern that I could explode because of a minor accident. Are there any cases of this happening? Why did Land Rover move the fuel tanks?

Petrol is dangerous wherever you keep it. The current 90 LR still has the tank under the seat. With a tank at the rear and a rear end impact, which is statistically more probable than a side impact, there is a greater risk of rupturing the even bigger capacity tank.

The risk of explosion is no greater than in the average car. If the thought still bothers you then consider running a diesel as the fuel is far safer to store, carry and handle.

Could you please advise me on a point regarding my Range Rover Turbo D, new in August of last year. There appears to be a gimmick on the throttle causing it to idle at some 1200 rpm when cold, although it drops back to 600 rpm when hot. An excellent idea, but it does mean too high a reversing speed, even in low ratio, for my liking with a trailer. Is there any easy way of temporarily over-riding this?

The idle speed normally drops quite quickly and should not cause a problem. It may not be adjusted or working correctly or as it is operated by water temperature, it may be air locked. It is not possible to over-ride the unit. As your vehicle is under warranty, I suggest getting it checked.

I want to buy a used 110 CSW and am committed to the V8, needing its on-road performance. However, I would like to minimise the fuel consumption

damage. With this in mind, I would appreciate any fuel economy tips you can offer and specifically:

1. Is there a particular year model I should seek/avoid?

2. Can the engine be adapted to use less fuel (e.g. R/R type fuel injection). If so, what might the adaptation cost be and who would do it? (I should point out that I could not bring myself to a Japanese option!)

3. Can you confirm that the Land Rover V8 will accept unleaded fuel?

4. What MPG range can I expect from the standard Land Rover V8?

1. There are really no bad models but windup windows are more user friendly and the five speed gearbox is more relaxed on long runs and is better on petrol.

2. It is possible but the improvement would not justify the cost.

3. Yes use with no adjustment and save money. It's cheaper than diesel at present!

4. Depending on use 18 to 23 mpg.

I run a One Ten V8 and advice on fuel consumption would be appreciated. You mention fitting SD1 carburettors and a Range Rover camshaft. What are the necessary part numbers needed to complete the job in one attempt? The vehicle is a 1989 model with 7,000 miles covered, could you offer a guess at the likely improvement in fuel consumption?

SD1 carbs are best sourced from a breaker's yard as they are readily available for about £25 per pair. A small overhaul and clean and they are ready to fit. The cam is part number ERC 2003. If your engine has a number starting 19g or 20g, it will be fitted already, but would benefit

from the SU carbs. To change the cam, you need a front cover gasket, inlet manifold gasket and two rocker cover gaskets. As yours is low mileage, the cam followers will be OK to use again. If the engine had done more work these would expect to be renewed as well. The expected improvement is approximately 3 mpg.

I have a Series III, two and a quarter SWB and I find it very difficult to start and keep going, even with the choke right out. Sometimes it can take up to eight miles before it is warmed up enough to stop having to keep a foot on the accelerator at traffic lights, etc. We have tried quickening the tickover which helps a bit, but sounds too fast. Once warmed up it's reasonably OK. Someone has told me that a new carb would help, someone else reckons the distributor would be best changed. What do you think?

It sounds from your description that the fuel mixture is too weak. This may be caused by a badly adjusted carb or a blocked jet within the carb or by an air leak from the manifold gasket under the carb. I certainly suspect the carb is at fault and a simple cleaning and retuning should cure your problems.

The Series IIA Land Rover that I own has a petrol engine with Solex carburettor. The Series III petrol engines have Zenith carbs. A lot of Land Rover specialists offer a Weber carb to replace the Zenith or Solex. Does the change of carburettor give so much of an advantage that the expense of about £70 is worthwhile?

The replacement of the carburettor is worthwhile if your old Solex or Zenith is worn out. The Weber does tend to slightly strangle the power under full load, but

Engine re-cons

does return better mpg figures in general use and is a good investment.

Does any firm specialise in supplying suitable reconditioned exchange cylinder heads to allow two and a quarter litre petrol engines to run on lead-free? What are the advantages?

The advantages are many. There is a decrease in the emission of toxic material from the exhaust and a lowering in running costs as unleaded fuel is cheaper in the UK than leaded. Many firms do them on an exchange basis. We can recommend Turner Engineering on 0342 834713 who supply them from stock or try the advertisers in LRO yellow pages.

I do hope you can help with a most annoying problem that recurs occasionally to my 86 inch Series One. In cold winter weather it develops a terminal misfire starting with a slight loss of power which slowly turns into a worsening, choking misfire eventually stopping the vehicle. The exhaust gasses are black at this point. If I switch off and wait about three minutes, she'll fire up perfectly and carry on sometimes ten miles further, sometimes fifty until the problem starts again.

Your problem is icing of the carb. In cold and damp weather the carb sometimes has difficulty in getting heat energy to vapourise fuel, so its temperature drops and it freezes the water droplets in the incoming air. This blocks up the jets and air passages in the carb leading to the engine stopping. If you leave the vehicle, the heat from the engine soaks into the carb and thaws it out for a few more miles. The cause is a faulty (or non-existent) thermostat not allowing hot water to circulate properly through the inlet manifold. The remedy is to renew the thermostat.

I have just replaced the Stromberg carbs on my 1975 low compression Range Rover with a pair of SUs from an SD1. These work fine expect for one annoying problem which I cannot seem to eliminate. When releasing the throttle after accelerating hard, or travelling some distance on a wide throttle opening, the vehicle momentarily accelerates before slowing down.

The most likely explanation for this is that the vehicle itself is not actually speeding up, but the cooling fan is! If your engine is fitted with a viscous coupled cooling fan and the viscous unit is faulty after running the engine fast for a short time and then slowing down the fan continues to spin freely and even speeds up. As most of the noise from an engine is from the fan this gives the impression that the engine has speeded up.

I have a 1982 Range Rover engine with Stromberg CD 175 carbs in my 1976 lightweight which I run on LPG or petrol. When I switch from LPG to petrol, the engine will not tickover at anything less than 2000 rpm. On LPG the tickover is fine. Secondly, I have problems with oil pressure building up in the front axle. The oil is getting into the wheel bearings and forcing grease past the oil seal and on to the brake shoes. I have checked the oil levels, repacked the bearings and replaced the oil seals. It has happened on both sides.

Solder the little spring loaded valves in the carb butterflys shut and it will tick over properly on LPG or petrol. There should not be any grease in the front wheel bearings, they are lubricated with the oil in the swivel housings. Replace the hub oil seals after checking the stub axle for damage where the seal runs and refill the swivel housings with oil. If the problem re-occurs then the seal between the axle and the swivel housing is faulty and allowing oil to pass from the axle into the swivel housing and then into the brakes. There are no breathers on the swivels but the axle breather must be clear.

I own a 1977 Series III vehicle with a 2.25 litre engine. The ignition timing is set to TDC for use with 2 star petrol, but this is becoming harder to find. For running on 4 star, should I reset to 6° BTDC?
No. Leave at TDC.

I have a Series IIA SWB petrol. It stands in the open and can be left unused for some time and is then required in a hurry! Although I have a brand new petrol pump and electronic ignition, it can still take some time on occasions to start, presumably to get petrol up into the carburettor. I am contemplating plumbing in an electric SU petrol pump, operated on a push button, to prime the carb only.

Would it be best to fit the electric pump in parallel with, or before or after (ie. in series with) the existing mechanical pump?
Your Land Rover may be fitted with either a Solex or a Zenith carburettor. If it has the Zenith then, if you are leaving it for a long period, try pulling out the choke after it has stopped. If you leave the choke out then the butterfly helps stop the fuel evaporating. If it has a Solex carb then this is probably worn out as they have not been fitted for many years. A new carb may cure the problem.

If you do decide to fit an SU pump, fit it either under the seat or bonnet depending on the type of pump you use and dispense with the original mechanical one as one

pump will have difficulty pulling fuel through the other.

I own a Series III SWB diesel. It goes well apart from one problem which has caused much embarrassment on more than one occasion. When I go down a steep or longish hill, braking on the engine, by the time I've reached the bottom the engine seems to be suffering from fuel starvation and consequently refuses to go up the other side. It takes much cranking of the engine with the starter motor to get going again — although the time it takes to fire up does vary. I have changed the fuel filter and bled the system. Any ideas?

I would also like to know how critical the timing of the distributor pump is, as I have tried adjusting it (by trial and error) about a couple of degrees, with some improvement in performance, but do not want to take it too far.
Your vehicle probably has a faulty injector pump. Remove and have tested by a specialist company.

The setting is critical to avoid smoke and damage to the engine. Set with the pointer on the block in line with the scribed mark on the pump base.

I own a 1973 Range Rover which about six months ago started playing me up. It began by not going up hills and it was suggested it might be the fuel pump. I replaced it with a reconditioned Jaguar 4.2 pump, which made it fly. Then it happened again and I checked the fuel filter and discovered that is was contaminated. I replaced the fuel tank which was a poor state and pumped clean

Miles per gallon

petrol through the engine until it was clear. This cured it and I had the carbs tuned to perfection.

Then, on a long haul, it wouldn't go up hill or overtake on the flat. A mechanic said that the piston rings were damaged allowing the fuel mixture to bypass the rings causing loss of power and eventual damage to the carbs. What do you think as I fear that putting it right may be a costly job?

Problems with pistons and piston rings are usually accompanied by high crankcase pressures which cause oil to be blown out of the front and rear crankshaft seals and the dipstick tube and breather pipes. If this is not happening then I suspect fuel starvation. There is a filter on the inlet side of the fuel pump which may be partially blocked and obstructing fuel flow. The rubber diaphragm in the carbs themselves may be partially holed which gives similar symptoms to those described. I suggest you have someone take a look at it who can tell you the exact problem and not speculate as to probable causes and costs.

I own an 'H' registered SWB 2286cc petrol engined Land Rover and am dismayed at the fuel consumption — about 15 mpg. What can I do? Perhaps fit another engine?

Taking áge into account and the lack of accuracy possible when measuring miles per gallon, 15 is not a bad score! If you need better economy, fit a Land Rover 2286cc diesel. This will give 25-ish mpg. The engine will fit straight into your Land Rover with minor modifications to fuel lines and wiring and exhaust front pipe.

I own a Series III Lightweight. Is it possible to fit the 90/110 door tops as the metal runners keep rusting out. Also the carbs on the SD1 V8 engine take a long time to return to idle when you take your foot off the throttle. I have stripped the tops off and cleaned and re-oiled them.

The early 110 door tops will fit straight onto your doors with no modification required. The usual cause of this is the spring going weak on the little valve on the throttle butterfly. Remove the carbs and solder the little valve shut.

What is the situation with regard to leaded petrol? I have been told it will be phased out by next year and motorists will be fined for using it. Secondly, what are your views on "power plus" systems which allow engines designed to run on leaded fuel to function on lead free?

Don't worry, leaded fuel will be available for many years yet and its use will not be illegal. My views on these systems are open at the moment, but I must admit that, like many, I am dubious about the claims of many similar products. The real answer is to fit the valve seats suitable for lead free petrol as previously stated, either having your own cylinder head reconditioned or fitting an exchange head available now from many sources.

We own a 1989 Turbo Diesel 90 hard top. Two fuel injectors blew which made the engine crackle very loudly. It was repaired under warranty but recently we have noticed the engine crackles very loudly when we slow down after a journey of several miles. The injectors have been checked again and are OK, but the noise is puzzling.

The noise you describe is not uncommon with this power unit. It seems to be one of the valves sticking in its guide and the piston just tapping it as it reaches the top of its stroke. The noise starts as a light tapping and builds up to a louder noise then stops suddenly. It often does not reappear for many more miles. As I assume the first year warranty will soon be over, I suggest you have the problem investigated.

My diesel shorty is a terrible smoker. I have only had this vehicle for three months (1985 vintage) but have covered about 3000 miles and tried all of the adjustments to reduce its habit. The clock reads 30,000 miles and the distributor pump is adjusted to its maximum in an attempt to reduce the smoke, but I cannot stop it.

It would appear that the injector pump timing is set incorrectly. With the tooth belt drive as on your engine, this is quite common. Fit a new timing belt drive as it is about due for one, set accurately and the problem will hopefully disappear. Follow the workshop manual as the procedure is too long to explain here.

Occasionally, when pulling away in first gear, the engine in my 1971 Series III will die unless the clutch is depressed quickly. This seems to happen after a short spell off road. It will restart easily and rev fine when in neutral. After a few attempts it will drive as normal.

I assume your Land Rover is a petrol and, if so, the problem is probably dirt in the carb which is being disturbed when driving off road and blocking a jet or the accelerator pump. Try cleaning the float chamber out.

My 1979 two and a quarter diesel has been leaking oil from around the fuel pump and I had put this down to a leaky gasket. However, when I stripped the pump off the block, cleaned it and left it on the workbench, I noticed it had leaked a small amount of oil from a 1.5mm hole located near the back underside of the pump. The hole goes right through to the inner mechanism and was therefore the souce of the oil leak. Is this hole necessary for the diaphragm to work independent of the crankcase pressure fluctuations or is there some kind of seal missing or broken?

The hole is necessary for the pump to operate, but the lower side of the diaphragm should not be open to the crankcase. There is probably some wear in the pump body where the actuating mechanism is. A new pump is the correct cure.

My two and a quarter petrol 1981 SWB would have needed an expensive conversion to run on unleaded petrol so I am using Carbonflo instead. When new, consumption was 19.5 mpg so Fairey overdrive, free wheeling hubs and an electric fan were fitted giving 21.5 mpg on two star. Now, using Carbonflo, consumption is 24 mpg on unleaded and is improving. Another very real benefit is the greater power — a fact, not just opinion. A regularly travelled long straight hill has a road sign at the bottom, now, when passing it at 50 mph, the Land Rover tops on the hill at 44 mph as opposed to 39 on two or four star fuel. I am just a very satisfied user and have no connection whatever with the makers of Carbonflo.

The results of using Carbonflo are quite impressive in the short term. It will be interesting to see if in the long term the claims that this product prevents damage to valve seats etc. from using leadfree fuel are true.

Chassis

I have a 1967 Series IIA LWB station wagon with six cylinder engine. The rear end of the frame is bad. I am restoring it and considering upgrading it to 110 spec. What I need to know is:

1. If I assemble a rolling chassis with a V8, air conditioning, coil springs, full time four wheel drive and other things that go with a 110, can the 109 body be laid on that chassis.

2. Are the Land Rover 110 drive train parts the same as Range Rover drive trains?

3. Can I put 110 doors on a IIA body?

1. Yes. The cross members and bulkhead outriggers are in the same places and it fits straight on. At the moment new chassis are only available from the factory. There are no non-genuine 110 chassis.

2. No, but the engine and gearbox and front axle will all fit. If you use 110 spring pads, the RR rear axle will fit (it's not as strong as a 110) and you will need to have a propshaft made up.

3. Yes, if you use the 110 hinges and lock strikers.

I have a 1983 Range Rover 3.5 petrol engine number 15D03073A, chassis number SALL HAM V3AA139874. Could you tell me anything about this vehicle? It is a three speed auto. Would I get better fuel consumption by replacing this with a four speed auto box and if so how can this be done? I also have a loud clonking noise on selection of gears. What would this be and possible remedy. Finally, can the vehicles run on lead free or must I adjust the timing.

The vehicle was built as a four door right hand drive auto low compression, but the engine is a 9.35:1 (high) compression automatic engine fitted with Pulsair but not an electronic distributor. The four speed box would be more economical than the three speed and is a relatively easy conversion. However, the improvement gained for the cost incurred would mean a financial breakeven point of several thousand miles. If your gearbox became faulty, however, then it would probably be worth doing. The clonk may be several things, but is most probably the ball joint on top the rear axle joining it to the rear 'A' frame. No adjustment is needed for lead free fuel.

Could you help me to find the history of my SWB lightweight IIA, chassis number 23600870A? Is is possible to find its original military number plate as it's been reregistered with a civilian number? Would I be able to change back to the old registration plates?

The military registration number in the form of two digits/two letters/two digits (such as 12 AB 34) is usually stamped on the vehicle identification plate screwed to

the bulkhead in front of the passenger seat. If this is missing write to: Information from Records, DVLC, Swansea, SA99 1AN, who can give you the information (if they hold it on their microfilmed records). If you obtain its military number, then the Museum of Army Transport, Beverley, Yorkshire, may be able to tell you its military service history. I doubt if at present you can have it reregistered on an age related basis, but when you write to DVLC ask them at the same time. Certainly, you will not be able to use the vehicle's former military number plate on public roads.

I am rebuilding a 1955 Series I and would like to know more about it please. The number is 170600671.

Your vehicle is a 1955 Series 1 86" wheelbase right hand drive home market model.

Recently I purchased a Series III SWB petrol from a local salvage dealer. The vehicle had been stolen and recovered and the number plates have been

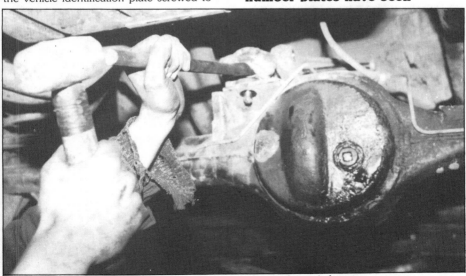

Replacing a Range Rover's ball joint which joins rear axle to A frame.

removed. **I wish to apply for the log book to retain the original suffix. The chassis number of the vehicle is 90168943A.**

The records for older vehicles are not held by Land Rover Ltd. Records are, however, held by the Heritage Trust 0527 854014. I suspect however that you have misquoted the number as the highest number I know is 57435. To establish that a vehicle has been stolen the Police must have a record of its reg no. Try to find from the salvage dealer the police station from which he collected the vehicle and enquire if they know its original number from their files.

Could you explain the differences between the chassis of a military Land Rover and a civilian one.

The military chassis is more heavy duty than the "civvy" one with heavier guage metal in places and deeper front spring hangers. It also has twin fuel tank mounting outriggers and usually (but not always) has a straight rear cross member instead of the angled type. The reason for this is the provision of lifting eyes on the edge of the cross member for lifting by crane or helicopter. The payload of the military 109 is one ton, the civilian 109 is ¾ ton.

Can you help me trace the history of my Land Rover? It's an ex-MOD SWB Series 11A, 2.25 petrol. Chassis number is 24114302B; engine number: 5117790B.

There is no year tracer in this series of chassis numbers but I suspect your vehicle was built in 1963. On vehicles of 1948 to 1970 there is a date tag on the top of the radiator. On early models this is a disc soldered to the top of the rad. On later models it is the tag which holds the rad cap chain and is thus marked 4M54, which means April 1954. If the original rad is still

fitted this gives an indication to the age of the vehicle.

I own a 1979 Range Rover, chassis number 35857365F, and have been told it is a right hand drive export model. Is this correct? I would like to change the distributor for the electronic type is it possible to fit new type instrument binnacle from 84/85 vehicle and also new type Vogue seats?

Your RR was originally produced as a left hand drive and was destined for Europe. The third digit "eight" means it was lhd if it had been "five" then it would have been rhd. It has been converted to rhd at some point after manufacture (as have many others, which if done properly is of no consequence). Lumination electronic ignition is probably the best to fit your RR or the later RR electronic distributor and power pack will fit your suffix "F" engine.

The later instruments will fit with wiring modifications but need the later type alternator fitted at the same time as this provides the signal to drive the rev counter.

The later seats will fit if you use the later mounts but you will have to modify the seatbelt mounts as they are fitted in the pillar of later vehicles. The rear seat is also mounted further back on different mountings. It may be easier to have your seats reupholstered by one of the specialist trim companies.

Wheels & Tyres

You consistently recommend fitting 7.50 × 16 Michelin XCL tyres to a Land Rover for road use. My local Michelin dealer tells me they are no longer manufactured. Do you have Michelin's address?

The address is Michelin Tyre PLC, Campbell Road, Stoke-on-Trent, Staffs.

I have found that over the years we have never had a problem with the Michelin tyres and they offer excellent value for money.

The best on road type is the XC type 4 as fitted on 110 vehicles, for more off road use the XCL offers good on and off road manners but is a directional tread pattern and has to be fitted the correct way round. The Michelin X type S is a sand type which is good on hard roads and sand but poor in mud.

Last November I bought a SWB diesel hardtop and it was shod with Michelin 6.50 × 16 radials. Being a forestry contractor and spending most of my time in woods and moors, I need a tyre with a lot more traction. I bought a set of BF Goodrich Traction Plus 7.50 × 16 LT cross plys. Now, after 9,500 miles, I wish I had gone for something else as there is only 3mm of tread left on each tyre all the way round. As 50 per cent of the mileage was off road, I am rather disgusted. What tyres would you suggest?

The Michelin XCL as used by the British Army, Camel Trophy and many others is probably the best tyre for your usage either in 6.50 × 16 or 7.50 × 16 form.

I run a 90 diesel on 205 × 16s for road use and Michelin XCL 7.50 × 16s for off road. However, when we all get snowed in this coming winter, what would you advise for a serious snow tyre? One of the above, perhaps, or am I better to buy a set of snow chains?

Lock limiting

The XCLs which you already have will perform well in snow without the use of snow chains. If the snow is deep (perhaps just wishful thinking by Land Rover owners) then no chain or tyre will help. The Land Rover will go easily through 9 or 10 inches of snow, but unless deeper snow is well packed, then the vehicle will not drive up on top of it and it builds up underneath bringing you to a halt. Chains, studs or snow tyres do not work at all then. The vehicles will go through deep drifts for short distances when the momentum of the vehicle will carry it through.

My 1972 SWB Series III is clad with 7.50 × 16 tyres and is used for getting to work and occasional horse box towing.

Do you think it would be OK to fit 9.00 × 16 tyres to improve road speed, and would they fit onto the standard wheels, which I think are 5 × 16, or will I need wider wheels for a good fitting.

Also could the later dual master cylinder, as opposed to the single piston one, now fitted (with or without servo), be put on without major surgery?

900 × 16 are not a practical proposition on a SWB they limit the lock and are just too big for the wheel arches. They will not fit the 5″ rims.

Fit the 7.50 × 16 as fitted to 110 for a better ride and tyre life from the radial tyres.

It is possible to fit the dual circuit systems as used on later vehicles if you use the brake pipes as fitted to the later models to get the circuitry correct. If you are not sure of what you are doing then leave alone to entrust to someone who does as 'mixing' brake components can have dire consequences.

I have just bought a SWB Petrol

Michelin XCL

Firestone SAT

Crossply or radial?

III although it was made in 1977 I don't think its had a very hard life, it has only 45,000 miles on the clock and going by its condition I think that's about right. The main fault I can find with the vehicle is the cab noise at speeds over 40 mph, (it will only do 60mph) I know the Land Rover was never meant for motorways but we plan on taking it on our holiday, is it normal for gearboxes to sound like they are going to fly out of the window or do I have a fault? The second thing that I would like to know is what happens if I put larger tyres on my vehicle, it has the standard crossply's at the moment. I have been told that fitting the larger tyres will give a better top speed, and a better ride, is that correct? If possible could you recommend a tyre to fit? While I do use my vehicle off road, I use it more on the road, what is the best type and size for general use.

Yes you do have a problem. General noise is usually a sign of a bearing problem. It may not necessarily be in the gearbox it could be a universal joint seized, a wheel bearing or many other items. A road test by a competent mechanic would confirm.

Fitting larger tyres 7.50 × 16 will improve the gearing and if radial tyres are fitted they will improve the ride as well.

My personal preference is for Michelin as I have had many years and miles of trouble free use from them.

I play to buy a Discovery 200 TDi and have two questions. Firstly, tyres. Having just returned from America where I drove a Jeep for about 70,000 miles on Goodyear Wranglers

Bridgstone Mud Dueler

Pirelli Scorpion

Noise penalty

(standard fit by Solihull to the Discovery), I was singularly unimpressed by them. About 60 per cent of my mileage in the UK will be off road and I will be towing a military style half ton trailer. Secondly, differentials, I have heard good things of the ARB air-locking diffs. Do you think they will provide a significant improvement in traction, especially as the cost of fitment would more than adequately pay for high quality winch gear.

My personal favourite for this type of work is the Michelin XCL. The 700 × 16 will fit the Discovery and are as fitted to the Camel Trophy vehicles 1990 in the USSR. There will be a slight noise penalty but as 60 per cent of your mileage is off road this should not be a problem. I have travelled thousands of miles on and off road and have never had any problem (other than the occasional nail) with Michelin tyres on cars or Land/Range Rovers so can recommend them from experience. The 110 we have, had its well known make of tyres replaced at less than 10,000 miles due to sidewalls breaking up (as have many others, with punctures from steel tyre cords penetrating the tube inside the tyre).

The ARB locking diff is an excellent device and will allow you to reach places with ease which may otherwise be difficult to get to. The answer would be to have both! The diff lock may affect the warranty on a new vehicle as at the moment they are not Land Rover approved fitments. If it was an "either or" situation, I would go for a winch as it could be used for other jobs such as moving fallen trees or recovering other vehicles etc.

I want to be able to secure the white eight spokes onto my SWB IIA, but cannot find a set of locking wheel nuts to fit. As far as I know they are the original studs, measuring 23mm across.

The best way to lock the wheels onto the vehicle is to change the hubs for later S2 or S3 with the larger studs. This is also advisable as the S1 and S2 studs were not designed to take wheel loadings. The load forces were taken by the centre hole in the wheel resting on the flange on the end of the axle. When fitting 8 spokes all the load is on the studs as it is with RR wheels and should only be used with the larger studs.

I have a Series III SWB Land Rover and the front hub (driver's side only) is losing oil. I've had the front hub off and checked it all, renewing the gasket but still it seems to be losing oil. I hope you can help as I don't really want to get the garage to sort it out as it will cost a small fortune.

I also wish to renew the suspension for something slightly better and would like to know what one you recommend and how easy it is to fit.

The oil may be leaking from the following points. Swivel housing oil seal, hub oil seal, the gasket between the drive flange and the hub or the felt washer on the end of the half shaft. Replacement of the offending item should rectify the problem.

LWB Stationwagon rear springs fitted to the rear of your SWB sill give the softer ride you are looking for.

Part Nos. 279678 and 279679.

On my 110 V8 County I use Goodrich Radial All Terrain T/A 31 × 10, 50 R15 LT M/S tyres during the summer. I use other types in winter. Do these tyres put an extra strain on the vehicle as they are bigger and probably heavier than Michelin 7.50 × 16. I am quite satisfied with the performance of the tyres but am

unwilling to use them if they are bad for my Land Rover in the long run.

The larger tyres will put more strain on the vehicle than 7.50 × 16, but the 110 can handle this increase without increasing wear or risk of breakage in normal use.

My Series III 109 petrol has recently started to eat tyres. I traced the problem to the fixing rivets inside the wheel rims which had rusted badly and were puncturing the inner tubes of the 7.50 × 16 Avon Rangers. Would it be legal to fit the military issue "run flats" to these rims. Also, where can I find military reflectors of the type found on military trailers?

It would be much easier to replace the wheel rims and use your original tyres than to use a run flat system. Alternatively, have your rims sand blasted and paint the insides with a rust resistant paint. There has been quite a lot of trouble with 7.50 × 16 Avon Rangemaster with the steel tyre cords breaking through the tyre to puncture the tubes, but we have not come across this with the Avon Ranger. The reflectors should be available from ex-military breakers (see ads in LRO).

I am fully rebuilding my 1974 Range Rover and would like to fit Vogue alloy wheels. Looking at the parts book, there seems to be two types of studs, one for steel wheels and one for both steel and alloy. Is it just a case of changing to longer studs?

Yes. Just change the studs to the later type. You may need to clean the flanges on the end of the axle shaft slightly with a grinder to allow the wheels to fit over. Do not pull them on with the nuts, but make sure they fit on their own first, then smear copper anti-seize compound onto the wheel face and centre before fitting.

Tighten the wheels to 90-95lbs ft (122-129 Nm) with a torque wrench.

I have a 1983 Series III V8 Safari in excellent condition. The vehicle is currently shod with Avon Ranger Mark II 750 × 16C tyres which are excellent for assessing our Scottish Hill lochs. I am considering retaining these but using 8 spoke rims with a tyre more conducive to 'road comfort'. What would you suggest? Secondly, in the September LRO you mentioned removal of the restrictors behind the carbs to achieve more power. Would this trigger any unpleasant side effects besides an escalation in the current consumption of around 16mpg. Lastly, is there a general problem regarding door locks on these vehicles? None of our door locking mechanisms work — am I just unlucky?

With tyres yer pays yer money and takes yer choice. I would recommend a 7.50 × 16 radial fitted to your own rims or to modestly wide eight spoke rims (I dare not tell you my preference or people will think I am biased towards Michelin).

The removal of the restrictors behind the carbs will actually improve fuel consumption and will cause no side effects.

There is no general problem with door locks, a spot of oil occasionally as a preventative measure stops seizure particularly in hostile environments such as winter salty roads.

I am in the dark about my red wheels. I have a green SWB 1959 Land Rover with bright red wheels. Is there a reason for this? Many people have suggested it might be a forestry vehicle.

If your wheels are "factory" red then they were originally fitted to a fire engine. As

Changing the spec.

the vehicle is 30 years old they have probably been repainted or changed in the past unless your L.R. was a fire engine. Look in the locker under the passenger seat for its original colour as it is usually not repainted in a respray.

I have previously used Michelin XCL tyres on a Ninety but have decided to fit Micky Thompson Baja Belted to my newly acquired One Ten County Turbo Diesel. I have fitted the 31/10.15 tyres to 15 × 7 rims. These wheels appear to have an offset of 4 inches. A standard Land Rover wheel is 4.75 inches. The tyre tread does not protrude beyond the wheel arch, but the side wall does noticeably. There is plenty of clearance inside the arch. Sinton Tyres recommended pressures of "about 30 rear and 25 to 30 front". This gives excellent performance on rocky and stoney tracks, comparable to XCLs. However, on road the steering is vague and the handling poor. The tyres are also noisy and thump. Please could you advise.

Fitting tyres and wheels with specifications different to the vehicle's originals can often lead to problems. For example if the centre of the wheel is too far from the centre of the steering swivels then shimying. premature wheel bearing failure and poor handling may result. Low ply ratings or lower speed ratings than specified for a vehicle may break the law eg 750 × 16 crossply tyres on a Range Rover.

The combination of large tyre and small diameter rims with large rim width does not suit the "heavyweight" Land Rovers such as your 110 and leads to handling problems as described.

A more conservative size true radial tyre in a 16″ diameter and able to run at higher pressure would cure the problem but as you have already purchased them you may be stuck with them.

Load carried on centre boss

Range Rover alloy wheel

Electrics

I have a 1962 Series IIa 2.25 litre diesel, positive earth Land Rover. Recently, the electrical system burnt out and now requires rewiring. Is it possible to convert it to a Series III negative earth electrical system including alternator, removing the two existing 6V batteries, fitting two 12V batteries to be run off a split charging unit? If so, where can I get hold of a wiring loom and split charging unit as well as the necessary wiring diagram. Is there any problem in fitting two 12V batteries?

Use the wiring loom fitted to the later IIa. These were negative earth and will fit your vehicle. As this has a dynamo system replace with an alternator. Connect the two 'A' terminal wires to the 'F' terminal wire on the regulator box wiring, insulate the other wires and tape up. Connect the small terminal wire on the loom to the warning light terminal on the alternator and the large dynamo terminal to the large output connector on the alternator.

Alter the main battery leads to use the front battery to start and run the vehicle and wire the battery under the seat to a split charge relay to take your auxiliary power for a caravan.

The wiring loom part numbers depend on the total amount you have burnt out as there are separate dash harness, dynamo harness, frame harness, engine harness and rear cross member harness. See ads in LRO for a supplier of your loom who is close to you or does mail order.

Could you please help me with the rewiring of the brake pressure warning lamp of my 1980/1 Safari six cylinder? What do the four terminals on the switch connect to? The originals were cut before I purchased the vehicle and I cannot find the answer on any wiring diagram.

Convert to negative

The four terminals from the top are: Black with a white tracer, white, black with a white tracer and black. The pure black is an earth, pure white is an ignition live feed and the two black with white tracers go to either connection on the brake failure warning switch.

My 1963 IIA 109 station wagon is suffering with charging problems. I end up with a flat battery about once a week even though the dynamo, heavy duty battery and voltage regulator have been replaced. I have heard of Land Rover owners converting to negative earth alternator system. Could you please describe what's involved in the change over.

After disconnecting the battery and removing the dynamo replace the dynamo with the alternator. It is possible to space the rear mounting bolt to suit the shorter unit but a more satisfactory job can be made by replacing the mounting bracket on the block with the later alternator type. Connect the large wire and small wire from the dynamo to the similar sized terminals on the alternator. The regulator box wiring must now be disconnected and the three large wires connected to each other (A, A1 and D) and insulated from the bulkhead. Use proper connectors such as the screwed block type as all the alternator output is through this joint.

Connect the small wire F (field) to the small wire WL (warning light) and insulate. Discard the E (earth) wire. After swapping the connections on the ammeter and on any radios, C.B. etc. then replace the battery terminals on the opposite battery posts. Use new terminals or swap the terminals on the wires to avoid confusion in the future.

How can I reduce interference on the radio in my 1981 Range Rover from the wiper motor? My vehicle has covered 62,000 miles

and the oil pressure when cold is 40 psi and 20 psi when hot. There are no obvious signs of engine wear though a small puff of smoke exhausts following a warm start. Could this perhaps be inlet valve stem oil seals? On a recent trip with caravan the vehicle used about 500 ml of oil in 188 miles.

The RR wiper motor is mounted in rubber bushes where it is screwed to the bulkhead. Later vehicles have a braided earth lead running to the body a few inches from the motor. Check your earth does this. Try feeding the radio from a supply which is on a separate circuit to the wipers.

The V8 engine does not normally consume oil. This puff of smoke, which is a common RR phenomenon does not indicate valve stem seal failure as seals are not fitted! Check that the flame traps on the top of the engine are not blocked and the engine air intake filter on the back of the engine is clear as problems in the engine breathing system can lead to oil consumption when working as described.

Nick Dimbleby wrote an article on police Range Rovers. He mentioned that a special piece of equipment was a split-charge alternator of 133/65 amp output. I have attempted to find out more about this alternator, but both Land Rover UK and Lucas Electrical were unable to help. Such an alternator would be of great use in a motorcaravan conversion I intend doing on a V8 Land Rover.

The 23 ACR alternator as found on the V8 SDI car will suit your requirements. Use with a split charge relay (part number RTC 8977) it is very similar to the police spec unit but more readily available.

An effective alarm

Can you help me with an electrical problem? With the vehicle standing still, both the temperature and petrol gauges on my SIII lightweight work perfectly, either at tickover or high engine revs. However, as soon as I drive off the temperature gauge falls to cold and the fuel gauge reads about half what is in the tank. I've replaced both gauges and the voltage stabiliser with no effect and I can see no reason for this problem. One suggestion is the cold air may be blowing over the guages affecting their readings — a long shot, I guess, but have you any ideas because after so long I've about run out.

The long shot is probably correct. The instruments work using a hot wire internally. As both gauges are affected look for holes in the bulkhead which will leak air onto the dash panel.

My 1958 SWB SII Truckcab is sadly in need of a rewire. Can I buy an off the shelf loom; which side of the engine do I mount an alternator as I would like to raise it above the dynamo position which is too near any deep water; is it possible to fit halogen headlamps. Finally I have been given a gearbox with the number 26107266 on top, 22 stamped on the right between gearbox and transfer box and Marshall 219467 on the side of the transfer box. Any ideas.

Wiring looms are available from many suppliers. Try the LRO "yellow pages". Fit the alternator in the dynamo position as water will not harm it. 7" halogen headlamps will fit directly if you replace the plug on the wiring loom behind the lights.

It is a series two box.

I have recently purchased a 1978 24v Army lightweight Land Rover, and would like to convert the ignition system back to 12 volt. I have had trouble finding out good details about what is needed and how to tackle the job.

The best thing to do with a 24v Land Rover is a compromise. Leave the vehicle electrics at 24 volt but replace the distributor and leads with normal Land Rover ones. This makes spark plugs affordable but retains the beauty of good lights and starting. Connect the coil to the voltage reducing box the same as the original coil with the screened leads.

I'm the proud owner of a Series III SWB Petrol Land Rover, but I wonder if you could give some advice on a really effective alarm system that I could fit myself, also I didn't want to fit the hasp and staple type of bonnet lock, but the type that I have seen fitted to some County and Ninety models, is that possible.

The best alarm is one that goes 'WOOF' and lives on Pedigree Chum!

Seriously though the best thing is not to put temptation in front of people and not leave expensive items such as cameras and tools in the vehicle. An inexpensive alarm can be made by fitting courtesy light switches to the doors and connecting them via a relay to the horn. Fit a concealed switch to isolate the system from outside the vehicle.

The 90 type lock will not fit the SIII bonnet.

I recently bought a Series III 1979 lightweight with 19,000 miles on it through the British Army auction here in Hong Kong. I changed the 24V system to 12V and wonder where I can get a 12V dial with water temperature, oil temperature and

Nato wiring

fuel level on it. Also, I have a square heater with doors on the side for which I need a 12V motor. Any suggestions?

These are available from many breakers in the UK. Try PRB Services, Leeds on 0532 796039 or Valley Motors on 0538 308352. This type of dial is mainly fitted to ex-MOD but the heater fan is common to Series II civilian heaters.

How easy would it be to fit a Series III dash (complete) to my 1974 Series III lightweight. Also, why do so many franchised Land Rover agents give the impression that they would rather sell complete vehicles and not bother about spare parts?

It is quite easy to fit a Series III civilian dash assembly into Series III air portable Land Rover. If you purchased the pieces from your local Land Rover 'graveyard' you should be able to copy the dashboard mounting brackets and heater duct. When I last did this I also used the civvy wiring loom and column shroud as this facilitated a change from 24v military to 12v civilian spec.

In reply to your second question, most Land Rover Parts dealers do not stock parts for vehicles of military origin. Most military vehicles have different springs, shock absorbers, lights, water pumps, fan belts and, more noticeably, body panels. You would be better dealing with an ex-military spares specialist (see the ads in LRO). Additionally, many parts are continuously changing part numbers or are being superceded by different parts. For example, a Series II propshaft U/J is now an RTC 3291, but has also been known as a 43023 and a GUJ116. A Land Rover Parts dealers' computer will only recognise RTC 3291.

I have a IIA converted to negative earth and would like to

fit an alternator. What sort and how do I go about this? Will the existing pulley, belt and mounting be OK? What about the voltage control box and do I need to change the ammeter?

The alternator can be fitted straight to your engine using the Series III mounting bracket but needs a Land Rover alternator pulley. Connect the large wire at the dynamo to the large terminal on the alternator and the small wire to the small spade terminal. Remove the voltage regulator box and connect the large wires A, A1 and D together. Ignore the E (earth) wire if fitted and join the WL (warning light) to the thin wire on the F (field) terminal. All this should be carried out with the battery disconnected. The ammeter can be left in but may show full deflection if the battery is in a very discharged condition.

I have just purchased an ex-army Series III ambulance with a trailer. I need to know the wiring for the Nato socket as I intend to use it for towing my caravan, but will need to alter the wiring to suit or obtain another Nato plug and add the 12n/12s plugs to this.

The wiring for the 12 pin Nato socket is as follows:

Pin numbers B and J stop lamps; pin K auxiliary; pins C, A and H convoy; pin E tail light; pins D and L earth; pin F spare or rear foglight; pin N righthand flasher; pin M lefthand flasher.

The wriring scheme is the same for 12v or 24v, but the bulbs used on the trailer differ with the application.

Transmission
Steering and Suspension

I use my 1972 109 daily in the building trade. However, the leaf springs, especially the rear, are horizontal when fully laden. I wish to renew with springs that will take reasonable loads yet be more comfortable to ride. I also need more ground clearance. What do you suggest?

Improvements to the springing can be made by fitting stationwagon springs 279678 and 9 as mentioned in previous answers but this will not increase the ground clearance as the clearance under the axle is not altered. Larger tyres are the only way to increase this. The maximum size on a 109″ is 900 × 16.

Having recently purchased a 1956 Series One 2 litre, I have noticed a lot of wandering and vagueness in the steering. The steering box was recently overhauled and new track rod ends fitted to the steering

linkages. This has improved it, but only marginally. Would the situation improve with the fitting of 205 radials on new rims, as I'm sure the present 'thin' rubber can't be helping at all.

The wandering is probably caused by a worn steering relay unit, mounted in the front crossmember. Replacing the tyres will not help if this is faulty but will improve the vehicle generally. They will fit SWB rims.

I have just purchased one of the very last (1985) Series III, short wheelbase, diesel Land Rovers. This has a damaged gearbox and overdrive unit. Is it possible to fit the Ninety gearbox to this vehicle.

The Ninety gearbox will not easily fit your LR without major modification. Refit Series III gearbox and overdrive.

I own a 1976 SWB Series III which is leaking oil from the seal

Leaky overdrive

round the offside swivel pin housing. As the housing is not pitted I cleaned it and replaced the seal, however it is still leaking some oil. Can I avoid renewing the housing by substituting thick oil to prevent further leakage?

If the surface of the swivel housing is not pitted and a new seal has been fitted, then oil should not leak. Check that the hub is correctly assembled as if, for some reason, it is not central on the swivel housing, oil can escape. Use of oil other than EP90 is not recommended.

To improve ride on my 88 I have taken your advice and fitted LWB station wagon rear springs part numbers 279678 and 9. With the 225 × 75 × 16 MS radials the ride is much improved. Can I now replace or modify the very rigid eleven leaf springs on the front?

There is no instant cure or replacement. A considerable improvement can be achieved by removing the front springs individually, placing in a strong vice and slackening the center bolt, undo the vice to reduce the tension allowing the leaves to separate slightly. "Butter" the leaves with grease and reassemble. This reduces the interleaf friction and thus softens the ride.

I have a 1964 IIA SWB and have fitted a secondhand overdrive. It uses about a pint of oil every 200 miles — is this normal?

The overdrive unit on your LR should not use oil. Unless the unit is leaking through the external gaskets then the oil is passing through the main oil seal into the transfer box and probably causing that to leak due to being overfull. Removing the unit and overhall would seem to be required before seizure occurs.

I have a 1974 109 Safari with 6 cylinder petrol engine. I have fitted a complete set of new springs with Monroe Gas Magnum 4 × 4 shock absorbers, but when viewed from the rear, the vehicle has a definite lean to the left. Any suggestions? Also, where can I get a top quality, chromed Union Jack badge and roller radiator blinds.

The part numbes for the springs for your L/R are NSF 264563, OSF 265627, NSR 279679, OSR 279678. (The numbers of springs are stamped on the underside of the 3rd or bottom leaf.) Check that these are correct and fitted to the correct corner. If all these are in order than see if anyone has replaced any of the chassis outriggers in the past (as for the some reason 6 cyl station wagons suffer more than their fair share of chassis rust) and that they have been replaced accurately.

Enamel union jacks are available from Barry Hatton International 021-353 1013.

I have not seen any roller blinds for some years, but it is possible to blank off most of the radiator grill during the winter either with a radiator muff or a piece of aluminium behind the grill and not overheat the engine.

I own a 1968 IIA Station Wagon and I have a problem with the overdrive filling up with oil. The oil seems to be coming from the transfer box, not from the main box. The overdrive was fitted in June 1986 and the leak began to show a few weeks later on a routine service. F.W. Winches provided a replacement unit and I was advised to fit a breather pipe to the transfer box, top inspection cover, to relieve excess pressure. The trouble started again a few weeks later and yet another overdrive was fitted, this one with double oil seals, but the oil leak was still there. Perhaps the gearbox to transfer box oil seal is faulty, but when I check the oil levels a few weeks after filling to the correct levels a small amount is missing from the main box, a much greater amount from the transfer box and the overdrive is full or near full.

Having changed the overdrive three times, and as this is not a common problem, we can dismiss this as being at fault. The main box is not draining through the seal into the transfer box, so this seal is not faulty. The most likely causes are, either parking the vehicle for long periods facing up a steep hill when oil is seeping past the seals into the overdrive unit, or I suspect that you are overfilling the transfer box. On Series II this is easily done as they have a separate filler and level plug.

The filler is on top of the box on a small square plate just in front of the hand brake drum. The level plug is some three inches lower and is a ¼ inch square plug on the back of the transfer casing, hidden by the overdrive unit. If you follow the instructions for later Series II and Series III and fill the box until oil starts to spill from the filler, then it is three inches too full *unless* you have the small level bung out.

If the box is overfull, then the overdrive seals are having to cope with excessive quantities of oil and are not doing so.

Can you tell me if a Rover SD1 four or five speed gearbox will fit in a Series III diesel.

The SDI gearbox will not fit directly into a SIII but may be fitted with the transfer box conversion as supplied by Ian Ashcroft 0582 761081 or by converting your transfer box and mounting it remotely behind the main gearbox. If you use with a four cylinder Land Rover engine you will need the 90-110 four cylinder five speed bell housing, clutch and spigot bush.

My Land Rover is a 1983 SWB Series III County station wagon.

I notice that the steering does not have such good self centring action as previous models I have owned and requires more steering on the road. This model was fitted with radial tyres as standard and is currently on 205 × 16 Michelin XM + S. When jacked up the steering is not stiff. Is this a characteristic of a Series III on radials or do you think there is something wrong? The Land Rover also has a hot starting problem. If left for more than about 20 minutes after a run, it takes several turns of the starter before it fires. it always starts but I feel there must have been fuel evaporation.

Land Rovers do not self centre very much because in common with most beam axled four wheel drive vehicles they do not have much of a caster angle on the front axle. I suspect the vehicle has a worn steering relay or other steering component allowing the vehicle to "wander". The radials actually increase directional stability.

Try replacing the one way valves in the fuel lift pump. An inefficient lift pump can often take several revolutions of the engine if hot and left standing for a short time. When the engine is cold and there is no vapour lock in the pipe the pump will deliver the fuel more easily.

I am planning to convert my Series III LWB 1974 diesel into a 6 × 6. The present axle is made by Salisbury and I would like to fit another driven Salisbury axle on to my vehicle. I wonder if you could tell me who could supply parts for the output differential to the second rear axle. I would also like to fit a Ford York six cylinder diesel into the vehicle. Have I to cut the oil sump of this engine?

Leaning to the right

The cost of converting to a 6×6 is prohibitive. The drive-through lockable centre axle costs more than your vehicle. If you need to go to a six wheeler the performance is still impressive in 6×4 configuration with a trailing dead axle. This performs better than pushing a dead middle axle. If you use a SWB rear axle with the diff hole blanked off, the SWB springs will run within the LWB ones.

The six cylinder York engine is best left in an 'A' series unless it has the Bosh injector pump as they are poor starters and gutless. If you fit it, the sump will need cutting at the front and deepening at the rear to maintain capacity.

After recently having an exchange engine professionally fitted to my 1980 Range Rover, I decided to completely renew the suspension using heavy duty front and rear springs 'G' on front 'Y' on rear and four new shock absorbers. After about a week, I noticed the vehicle had settled about 15mm more on the off-side — noticeable on a level surface. It seems to me that the problem is coming from the front off side spring settling 15mm more than the rear. Being someone who hates anything that's not as it should be, it is driving me crackers. Please help.

There are several reasons why Range Rovers lean and your lean of 15mm is not great as leans go! If you fit heavy duty springs which raise the ride height, then the vehicle is more prone to leaning. I am unsure which springs you have fitted. the 'G' and 'Y' are not part numbers. The number for heavy duty front springs is NRC2119 (these are actually standard rear as well). Try substituting the original springs and if the lean disappears, buy the correct new springs if you still want them.

I own an ex-Irish army Series III

1972 Land Rover. I've recently fitted a Range Rover V8 instead of the 2.25 and would like to know if I can put a transfer box on to a 5-speed SD1 gear box.

Yes you can. The only person who does this conversion is Ian Ashcroft, 0582 761081.

I am considering fitting an overdrive unit to my 1983 SIII SWB and would like to know the likely improvement in mpg. I have also fitted 750×16 tyres — how does this affect calibration of the speedo and mileometer. I understand that the readings are only correct with standard tyres.

There is only a marginal improvement in fuel consumption with an overdrive, but the vehicle is much less stressed at cruising speeds. The likely extra mpg is 2-3.

Your speedo needs changing for a LWB or recalibrating by a specialist company. The fitting of 7.50×16 tyres in place of 600×16 gives an increase of about 11 per cent to the gearing. As, by law, a speedo needs to be correct to within 10 per cent. then it would now be illegal with the addition of larger tyres (assuming, of course, that the speedo was accurate in the first place).

The fitting of an overdrive does not alter the speedo reading as the ratio change is before the gearbox output shaft where the speedo drive is situated. Changing diffs, however, does. If you put Range Rover 3.54:1 differentials in a Land Rover, then the increase in gearing is 25 per cent and so the speedo reading is well below the actual speed and well outside the legal requirements.

The ratio change is worked out like so

$$\frac{4.7 - 3.54}{4.7} = 25\% \quad \frac{\text{(ie, original} - \text{new)}}{\text{original}}$$

I have a 1983 One Ten V8 (4 speed) and I am considering fitting an overdrive. Can I buy

an overdrive for a Range Rover (there's so many discount offers in the mag) or get a used one and make the linkage myself?

First and second gear are nearly impossible to shift up and down, or from third to second for the first two miles in winter. Any ideas?

The cheapest way to increase the gearing on a One Ten 4 speed is to fit the Range Rover output gears in the transfer box. They are FRC 4050 and FRC 4032. (This also applies to the Stage 1 V8). It sounds as though you may have selector trouble. Sometimes the reverse gear flap spring can come off and jam the selectors, or one of the roll pins which hold the selectory together can move. It may also be trouble in the 1st/2nd syncromesh. A strip down will tell you. If it is selector trouble this is often possible to rectify by taking the top off the gearbox in situ. Check also the oil in the box is engine oil not EP90.

I have fitted an SDI car engine to my Range Rover. It runs

perfectly but the clutch will not disengage. I have used the Range Rover flywheel and clutch assembly which was OK before the engine swap.

You have obviously used an automatic engine. This has a spigot bearing the same size as the Range Rover but made of steel and not phosphor bronze. The bush welds itself to the primary shaft and will not disengage. Remove the engine (with difficulty) and replace the bush with the correct bronze one (549911).

I wish to alter the low range gearing in the transfer box to something lower than is already fitted in my V8 109 and would appreciate a "crawler" gear. Does anybody make pinions which I can use to put into the transfer box to replace the existing ones?

The 109 V8 shares the same low range stepdown ratios as all four speed Range Rovers, 110 V8 and 101 forward controls. In most applications first gear low box is low enough. If you need to lower the

Overdrive fitted to SII gearbox.

Power steering

gearing the only way would be to reduce the tyre size to 205 × 16 or similar and fit Range Rover high range transfer gears or overdrive to restore a respectable road speed.

I have recently become the owner of a 1980 88 inch Series III with a genuine 17,500 miles from new. The vehicle tends to wander a lot and, with a caravan on the back, is even worse. The tyres are the original 6.00 × 16s pressured at 25 psi in the front and 30 psi in the back. All mechanical parts seem in very good order and the vehicle has not been in any accidents. It has never been off road.

The Land Rover does tend to wander on 6.00 × 16 crossplies. The 205 × 16 radial tyres (as on Range Rover) help in this respect. There may be a problem, however, with the steering relay having siezed from lack of use. 17,500 miles in ten years is hardly excessive and whilst standing inactive, the relay through the front chassis crossmember may have tightened up. Remove the grille and one of the 7/16 AF spanner size bolts on top of the relay under the battery carrier, dribble oil for a small can into the bolt hole and into the relay. The relay will usually free up after a couple of doses of light oil in this manner.

I have a 1988 turbo diesel 90 County. The power steering pump is giving me problems. A noise at 44,000 miles turned out to be the early warning of a catrastrophic failure as, over the next 4,000 miles the rollers chewed their way 5mm into the front pump housing causing a gradual loss of power steering. My concern that this might be a common fault was raised when I quoted the part number to my local Genuine Parts dealer who

not only instantly recognised it, but knew how many were in stock and which bin they were stored in — and all without consulting the stores computer. Was I just unlucky or are Land Rover's power steering pumps not up to much?

Secondly, I would like to install a tachometer, is there anyone who can supply me with an add on unit that could be attached to the Lucas A127 series alternator?

The failure of the PAS pump is quite a common occurence, so you are not alone. I am unable to find a supplier of an add on tachometer. The vehicles which use this system have the units built into the pod, such as the Rover SDI 2400 diesel and the Range Rover.

What grade of oil should I be using in the main and transfer boxes of my 1972 Range Rover? When I first bought the vehicle five years ago I noticed gear oil in the boxes. However, although the original handbook recommended this type of oil, a supplement sheet stipulated 20W/50 oil (engine oil). I have followed the latter directive but I am not convinced it is the best for the vehicle — shouldn't engine oil be used for engines and gear oil for gearboxes? Furthermore, the temperature generated in the gearbox is quite alarming, especially when towing a caravan, a fact noted when you place your hand on the gearbox console inside the vehicle. I understand the gearbox is designed to run at a temperature of 95 °C, so would it not be prudent to use the heavier oil?

Your are using the correct oil in the gearboxes. The main gearbox has an oil pump to circulate the oil unlike most gearboxes designed at that time which relied on splash lubrication. When the gearbox is cold the pump will not circulate thick oil and premature failure of bearings etc. will result. The hot transmission is normal; it is great in winter, as the car has central heating without the need of a blower fan, but in summer it can sometimes be a problem keeping the driver's feet cool. The heat is from thermal transmission from the engine, the exhaust, which runs close and frictional losses within the boxes themselves.

Can I replace the worn out gearbox in my Series III two and a quarter petrol with a Series II box? They have a better reputation for reliability.

The units are totally interchangeable if you use the SII clutch mechanism and SII cover.

I own a 1969 IIA petrol Land Rover and my problem is that, when I use four wheel drive, I get a knocking from the front wheels when turning. I have been told by the previous owner that he filled the hubs with grease instead of oil. Is it easy to dismantle and what is knocking?

The last owner of your LR has filled the front hubs with grease because the front swivel oil seal is faulty and would let oil leak out. Replace this seal (the large seal which rubs against the chrome swivel) and the universal joints in the front drive shafts and the problem should be solved. The practise of putting grease in the swivel housings should be avoided as this does not travel up to the front wheel bearings and leads to their premature failure.

I understand that Series III gearboxes came in two different gear ratio sets, the later one with a fourth gear ratio of 0.792:1. Can the standard Series III gearbox be fitted with the second set (overdrive variant) of gears? Also, can a Series III gearbox be installed in a Series IIA?

I am afraid you have been mininformed. All fourth gear main box ratios are direct, or 1:1. A Series III box is a direct replacement for a Series II if you use the Series III clutch cover and release bearing. It is of dubious advantage however, as the Series II box is stronger.

I own a 109 Safari and it is ex-military with the two and a quarter petrol engine. I would like to know if the machine can be converted to full time four wheel drive.

There are no real advantages to permanent four wheel drive but, if you wish to, use the transfer box from a 1948-50 Series One. This is permanent four wheel drive with a free wheel overrun clutch in the front output to stop transmission wind up. It will, as a unit, swap with your transfer box. If you use the latter box, it even has a yellow knob to lock the box in four wheel drive for reverse. The modification is easy, but the benefits are questionable.

When I try to move the prop shafts by hand the front one moves freely by about 10 to 12 degrees and the rear one about 6 to 8 degrees. If I accelerate hard then release the throttle suddenly, the transmission makes a clunk. Can you help me?

Free play of this amount is quite normal in the axles. I suspect the noise is either in the transfer box or in the suspension bushes, or in the balljoint on the rear axle "A" frame.

The gearbox in my 1973 Series III two and a quarter petrol is noisy and jumps out of third gear. I have recently reconditioned a SIIA gearbox. Will it fit?

Extended shackles

Yes, the gearbox is a direct replacement if you use the SII clutch release mechanism and SII clutch cover. The lack of syncromesh on second gear is the only significant difference.

I own a Series III 109 inch diesel Australian import Land Rover, chassis number 523759, which is fitted with nine leaf front springs. Why is this? Secondly, is it possible to fit extended shackles to the rear of the front springs as I have seen on some military LWB? Is it possible to fit heavy duty HCPU 110 rims to this vehicle?

UK specification 109 diesels are fitted with eleven leaf front springs, the nine leaf being a petrol engine spring. It suggests that your vehicle was once petrol engined or has had the wrong springs fitted at some point. If there is sufficient clearance between spring an bump stop, then leave alone, but as you ask about extended shackles, I suspect the axle is up to the bump stops. If so, fit the eleven leaf springs (o/s 265627 and n/s 264563). The military type shackles will fit your Land Rover and are probably best sourced from a Land Rover breaker as the last time we purchased new they were virtually impossible to obtain. The 110 rims will fit straight onto your Land Rover. The normal rims are the same as SIII LWB, the heavy duty are the same as the old IIA and IIB forward controls and odd military fire engines, etc.

I have an ex-Belgian military SIII 88 inch Land Rover. At present it is only two wheel drive. How can I turn it back into a 4 × 4?

Replace the front axle complete with a driven unit. Remove the transfer box from the back of the main gearbox and fit a normal transfer box. Join up with a front prop shaft. The rear axle of your vehicle may be fitted with a limited slip differential

but this should not cause any problems. The parts are best sourced from a donor vehicle, any SWB SII or III will be suitable. A LWB front axle may be used, but the brake master cylinder will need changing to work the brakes properly.

My Series III jumps out of first gear on over-run. An inspection has revealed nothing wrong. Could it be a weak detent spring? What do you think the problem might be?

The most likely cause is a worn 1st/2nd syncro hub. Which can only be seen when the gearbox is dismantled. If the detent spring is weak it would probably jump out of second as well as it utilises the same spring.

Is there a firm that can overhall the self levelling unit as fitted to the Range Rover?

At present, as far as I am aware, there are no companies remanufacturing the self levelling unit. There are many selling good second hand units, however, which is the only alternative to a new unit in the case of failure.

I am running a 1986 V8 County 90 which at 25,000 miles has no more than normal backlash in the transmission line, yet a most irritating noise has developed which can only be described as a clunk that occurs whenever I apply or lift off the throttle in any gear.

Without inspecting the vehicle it is hard to locate a noise, but the most likely cause is a worn ball joint on top of the rear axle where it is located onto the rear suspension top links. To check this look at the top of the axle and, as someone moves the vehicle forward, watch to see if the axle top moves forward slightly. Wear may sometimes be detected by using a small pry bar under the joint, but on Range Rover and 110 with self-levelling suspension, the levelling unit pushes on the joint and can hide any play present. The joint is not expensive and only takes an hour to change.

I own a 1967 Series IIA LWB diesel and would like some advice. When in 4WD or front wheel drive only (rear half shaft broken) I get a snatching on the steering when at full lock at low speed. It is not something which presents too much of a problem, but it may be causing damage in the long term. In the past I have overhauled the king pins, etc.

The snatching is usual on full lock as the universal joint in each front drive shaft speeds up and slows down as it is not a constant velocity joint (unlike the V8 109 and Range Rover).

I've been overhauling the gearbox in my Series III 109, 4-cylinder petrol, but cannot find a trace of gearbox number to order parts. Can you help?

The gearbox number is located on the selector cover on the top of the main box stamped on the right hand side at the back. It is usually obscured by oil and mud but is just visible through the hatch under the middle seat.

I have an aggravating whine coming from my gearbox every time I decelerate in fourth gear. It is also present in third gear but much less so. The problem began when I converted my 4 × 2 to 4 × 4. The new gearbox, 57111504, had to be fitted with the 4 × 2 bell housing to mate to the 2.2 BMC diesel engine using a Phillips conversion kit. It also has reconditioned 4.3:1 diffs and drive shafts. I later removed the gearbox and re-placed all bearings and worn parts, still the noise. I shimmed the transfer box to the recommended tolerances, still the noise. I've

even tried Slick 50 and wearing ear protectors. Can you help?

This type of noise is often from a diff and travels down the tubular propshaft to sound as if it comes from the gearbox and gets louder as the roadspeed increases. As the diffs have been rebuilt I suspect the rear diff may be the cause of the noise. Remove the rear prop and half shafts (if it is a S2) after draining the axle oil to stop spillage a short run in front drive only will prove or disprove this.

Can I use "SLICK 50" in my 1959 SWB front and rear axles, transfer box, Fairey overdrive, gearbox and engine? My brother tells me it has improved his car's performance and fuel consumption.

This friction reducing additive may be used in all the engine and transmission of your L.R. with beneficial results.

I have an X-reg Series III SWB. Can you tell me why, on returning to normal drive after 4WD, I experience severe jumping in the steering action for a brief time before everything returns to normal. Also, using 4WD seems to cause a minor oil leak which again appears to be self curing after a period in normal drive. Finally, I have seen several references to transmission "wind-up" — what is this please?

When a four-wheel vehicle goes round a corner, the sum of the rotations of the rear wheels is different from the sum of the rotations of the front wheels. So, on a 4 × 4, unless the vehicle has a differential in the gearbox to allow for the different rotations of the front and rear propshafts, the transmission will "wind itself up". this causes severe tyre wear as the two axles are "fighting" each other, or failure in the transmission. If used in an off-road

Better cruising

condition in 4WD this will not occur because an element of wheel slip will take account of the differing rotations.

If "wind up" occurs then the gearbox will not usually come out of 4WD into 2WD until the wind up is "unwound". This "wind up" will show by the front tyres trying to skip and skid and steering feeling heavy and notchy. To "unwind" a vehicle when it is on a hard surface, just drive one front wheel briefly onto the verge and allow the wheel to slip slightly and the transmission to disengage itself.

Your oil leak, if on the gearbox, is probably the front output shaft seal. If this has been leaking for some time then the transfer box is probably low on oil. This may explain its reluctance to come out of four wheel drive.

I own a 1973 SWB, 2.25 petrol.

With overdrive, a comfortable cruising speed is 55-60 mph. However, I would like to boost this to 65-70 mph. Could you suggest a suitable power unit to a give this?

V8 Rover! With, depending on your tyre sizes, Range Rover 3.54:1 diffs and the already fitted overdrive.

The fuel consumption of my 1966 IIA two and a quarter petrol is horrendous and the oil consumption is not much better. I know Range Rover diffs can be fitted, but can a five speed Range Rover box be used with this engine? Would it improve fuel consumption? If not do you have any suggestions?

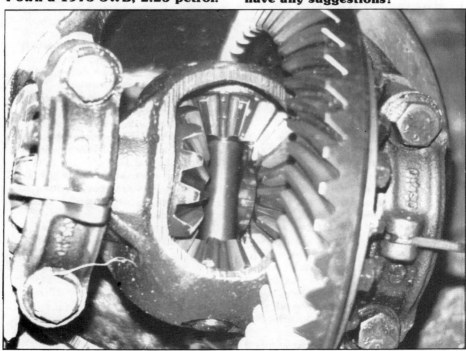

Range Rover differential.

The fuel consumption ought to be in the high teens/low twenties. If your engine is using a lot of oil it sounds as if a replacement or rebuild is required. A worn engine will use more fuel than a good one. The fitting of a five speed box will not improve matters and involves major reworking of the vehicle. Range Rover diffs will fit easily but, with a worn engine, will probably make the consumption worse than it is. Sort the engine out first then consider other fuel saving items later.

I have just brought a SWB Series III TC fitted with a high compression V8 from a P6 car and 255/85 — 16 tyres. The rest of the mechanicals are standard Rover. My problem is one of gearing — basically it is too low in all gears. I can pull away in all but top, which I can engage at walking speed, consequently cruising is very thrashy. It would seem that changing differentials is better than fitting an overdrive as it will broaden all four gears. Do you agree with this and will Range Rover 3.54:1 differentials fit in place of 4.7:1 Land Rover ones in Rover casings?

Range Rover diffs will directly interchange with your SWB Land Rover diffs with no modification. Replace both so that you can use four wheel drive. As you say, they will work in all gears, unlike an overdrive.

When checking the front drive shaft, I find the splines have a large amount of play or movement. This causes vibration when the hubs are locked in. I have been told that the only solution is to run with the hubs locked out all the time, but is there a better solution? Does the rubber boot have any effect? Why can't someone come up with a better boot than a rubber one?

Changing the front driveshaft will stop the vibration. The rubber boot is to stop ingress of dirt, etc. into the splines, causing premature failure. There is a facility on most shafts for greasing which if done (not overdone) regularly will minimise wear such as on your vehicle. If properly fitted to the shaft, the boot has a long life. If incorrectly fitted, it is soon ripped to bits with even gentle off roading.

Could you please advise me as to the cause of the problem I have with my 1988 2.5 petrol County 90?

Under warranty I have had two replacement gearboxes, a clutch assembly and a complete transmission change in under 5,000 miles, due to a rattle, seemingly in the gearbox when running light.

At first, each gearbox only started rattling with a warmed up engine but each got worse until the rattle could be heard with a cold engine on revving up when stationary. The noise disappears when the clutch is depressed. It is also hardly noticeable in 5th gear. With the diff lock in neutral and the main gearbox in any gear it is really bad.

With three gearboxes making the same noise it seems to me a design fault, but is there a cure?

The 5 speed Rover gearbox tends to chatter when running light, but without hearing yours it is difficult to say if it is louder than normal. The gear lever also chatters in its plastic cup, if it has not been replaced try that. There may be another problem which is manifesting itself by making the gearbox chatter such as an out of balance engine or faulty gearbox mountings. If you are still unhappy contact the Service Dept at the Land Rover factory.

Engines

After buying a 1969 IIA LWB safari with 2.25 petrol engine, overdrive and free wheeling hubs, I was also pleased to find a Weber carb fitted. However, fuel economy is poor and as I am planning to drive to Morrocco next year I am thinking of fitting a Ford V6 3.0 litre or 2.8 litre engine. What do you think?

Changing to the Ford engine will not do wonders for your fuel economy. Perhaps a diesel engine would be a better alternative as diesel is more readily available and cheaper in countries like Morocco. It is also safer to carry in cans and the engines are more fuel efficient.

I have recently replaced the much abused 2.25 engine in my 1975 109 with a Rover 3.5 V8 unit. I believe the engine was from a 1974 P6 3500S. The engine number is: 9.25:1CR 48108326(?) the last letter could be a D. Will this engine run on unleaded fuel. My local Rover main dealer says no. What is the truth?

The engine is indeed a P6 engine and as with all Rover V8 engines may run lead free.

Engines with higher compression ratios would be more suited to Super Lead Free petrol particularly the 10.5:1 compression P5 coupé engine as the high compression ratio will lead to preignition.

The highest compression engines as used by Land Rover Ltd need the timing retarding 3° to run satisfactorily on normal lead free. These engines are found fitted to later Range Rovers but not 90-110.

Could you please give me some idea of the practicality of converting an 88 inch Series III using the V8 Rover engine to an automatic. This is asked as an avid fan of Landies and being a disabled driver.

It is quite possible to fit V8 and Auto parts to a Land Rover either by mounting the transfer box further back remotely or by fitting an adaptor between the auto box and transfer box. The whole job needs a lot of re-engineering of the vehicle. Depending on your disability you may find a hand operated clutch which is easy to fit or an automatic Range Rover may be the answer.

I was very interested to read the letter from Mr. D. G. Shaw of Bournemouth, in the July LRO, regarding the fitting of a BMC 2.5 diesel engine in his vehicle. I have a 1977 Series II LWB estate fitted with the same power unit and would agree with his remarks about the speed and pulling power. However, I do have an overdrive fitted and this makes a world of difference — comfortable cruising speed is in the 45-50 mph region.

During the first few months of this year I made extensive fuel consumption checks and my overall mpg is 22.73. Most of the mileage was on tarmac roads with a few miles cross country and admittedly, I did not have to use low ratio at any time. So, my advice to Mr. Shaw would be to fit an overdrive unit, after the initial expense both he and his pocket will benefit.

Finally on the subject of the BMC 2.5 engine, do you know of any instruction manual, workshop manual or parts catalogue that is available for this unit? I have tried without success and the Haynes Manual only covers the standard Land Rover 2¼ Diesel Engine.

The BMC 2.2 and 2.5 unit was fitted to many of the Austin FX4 'Black Cab' — workshop manuals and part lists for these are available from many of the cab specialists who advertise in Exchange and Mart under "Taxi Spares" as are new and secondhand parts to fit these engines.

I am fed up with the power of the normally aspirated diesel engine in my '84 Ninety. Will the new diesel turbo in the Discovery fit the Ninety?
The Discovery engine will fit the 90 but will require an intercooler and much modification to cables, exhaust and pipework. The 90 Turbo engine is more powerful than the normally aspirated and will fit in more easily. If you need much more power then a large capacity turbocharged engine is required such as the Nissan 3.5 available from many suppliers who advertise in LRO.

I have recently fitted a Rover 2.5 V8 to my lightweight. The conversion went well and took me just over a week to complete. The engine is a P6 type with a manual lift pump and SU carbs with automatic choke. I have been informed that the auto-choke is a rather vintage type. My problem is fuel evaporation due to heat (I assume). The engine does not boil or run hot, around 85°-90°C (is this temp normal?) Can you suggest anyway to stop the fuel evaporating, retaining the original carbs, choke etc, as the vehicle runs very well until I switch off when warm. Then it becomes difficult to start. The vehicle starts after cranking on the starter, and runs perfectly until I switch off, and then the whole process has to be repeated. Both carburettors have been overhauled and then set up on a crypton machine.
Replacing the fuel pump with an electric pump such as a Facet as used on the Range Rover or SU as used on Jag XJ6,

Smokey start up

6 cylinder Land Rover and other vehicles will cure this annoying fault. Route the pipes well away from sources of heat such as the exhaust and cooling systems.

We have a home market, RHD, Series II 2.6 litre, six cylinder 109. Is it possible to re-bore the 2.6 litre engine to accept 3.0 litre pistons and sleeves from the Rover car engine?

The engine shares a common block with the 3 litre and the pistons are interchangeable but will give a slightly higher compression ratio. To go to 3 litres, change the crankshaft and con rods for the 3 litre items. It would be beneficial to change the camshaft as well to the 3 litre. All the parts interchange as it is basically the same unit.

When I start the two and a quarter petrol engine in my IIA 109 from cold, a cloud of light grey smoke is emitted from the exhaust when the engine first fires up. This lasts only a second or two. The engine is low mileage and runs extremely well. Any ideas what might be causing this?

The smoke is probably unburnt fuel. If the carb is a little bit worn it will do this. The Solex carb is more prone to this than the later Zenith. It may also be slight oil burning which is also very common as the engine starts and only happens for a few seconds. This is a "feature" of Land Rovers and is not really cause for concern.

I have just bought my first lightweight and have noticed some funny groaning noises from the floor area. It moans whether on the move or stationary. Help.

The moaning noise from military Land Rovers comes from the oil cooler system. They usually moan when the engine is low on oil or if the oil relief valve plunger

spring has gone weak. This is mounted on the top of the oil cooler between the union and the pipe. Removing the spring and replacing with a new one or sometimes stretching the spring cures the groaning noise. Whilst the groan sounds awful it is not actually detrimental to the operation of the vehicle.

Anyone considering buying a "Fully Reconditioned" 2¼ diesel engine and living in the north may care to listen to my all too true story.

About two years ago I had fitted, for an embarrassingly large sum, a secondhand diesel at a very reputable L/R specialist situated somewhere near the present end of the M65.

The engine gave every satisfaction until a few days ago, when with an enormous bang, the crankshaft broke. Inspection revealed that the crank had a very large "P" cast in a prominent place and was, you've guessed it, a petrol engine crank. This is a very nasty rip-off trick to play on the unsuspecting public as a petrol crank will last until well out of the guarantee period before giving up the unequal struggle.

The only answer to this, that I can think of, is to take the engine number of your intended purchase and check with Land Rover that this was never a petrol engine.

Is there a recognisable number sequence denoting "diesel".

The use of a petrol block on a diesel engine is not a problem as the parts are exactly the same. The problem is with the crankshaft. The diesel unit is of forged steel and carries a "D" stamped on the web of the crank. The petrol version, whilst sharing exactly the same dimensions is

V8 conversion

marked "P" and it is made from cast iron and will not run for long in a diesel unit — as you have discovered. Some military petrol engines however are fitted with the forged steel crank and these will fit and run in diesel units.

The starting nos. for 2¼ engines are as follows:
2286 P 8:1 cr 3 bearing 241 00001; 901 00001; 902 00001; 903 00001.
2286 P 7:1 cr 3 bearing 251 00001; 253 00001; 904 00001.
2286 D 3 bearing 271 00001; 906 00001.
2286 D 3 bearing 276 00001.

I hope to build a V8 Land Rover mainly to be used on road so mpg and mph are important, but it must sound and look great (wheels, tyres, etc.), do well off road and out perform my dad's new Land Cruiser!! Please could you give me some advice on model, diff ratio, tyres, etc. and initial purchase price.

The best ingredients for a V8 Land Rover are a good SDI engine and flywheel, Series II gearbox with overdrive, 3.54 diffs and Range Rover type wheels with 205 × 16 tyres. Take the brakes from the LWB 6 cylinder with servo and fit the whole lot together on a very sound chassis vehicle. An ex-military Series II or lightweight would be a sound basis and could be transformed into a good vehicle (see ads in LRO for a guide to purchase price).

Before starting such a project, check with your insurance company to see what they will cover.

I have a 1981 6 cyl 2.6 109 Hardtop and have recently acquired a good low mileage SDI V8 lump which I want to change to. I have spoken to a number of engine conversion kit suppliers and the almost unanimous response has been "ooooogh the 6 cyl, that's a difficult

conversion . . . it needs extensive mods to the bulkhead . . . or . . . the propshaft needs changing, the gearbox needs moving . . . etc."

I have taken engines out of cars, rebuilt them and then put them back, but I have never carried out a conversion before. I would be very grateful if you could list out the mods that are really required in order to carry out this job.

The 6 cyl is the best Land Rover to fit a V8 into as there is 6″ more room in the engine bay and the brakes are good enough for the extra power. The only modification on the vehicle is to trim the side of the footwells to allow the exhaust manifolds to fit. The prop, gearbox etc. remain as original.

You will have to fabricate an exhaust system or use the purpose built one available from Jake Wright (0943 863530) and make up suitable water hoses and throttle linkage. The oil filter will have to be replaced with an adaptor and remote filter fitted to stop the axle touching the filter.

The competent enthusiast should be able to complete the work.

I own a 1979 Series III SWB 2¼ diesel, which I use to commute 75-80 miles daily to work and back. Most of the run is via motorway and covered at an average speed of 50-60mph. Free wheeling hubs and Fairy overdrive fitted.

My problem has arisen where engine oil is emitted from the rocker box cover breather and fixing bolt mountings. New copper washers under the dome fixing nuts appears to have cured them but a new 'O' ring on the breather seat still allows the

Problems galore

oil to pass through and over the engine. Oil does not appear to be emanating from either the filler cap or the dip stick tube and no obvious cause is apparent. It would appear that the rocker cover is becoming pressurised and oil consumption is approximately one pint per 150-200 miles.

The engine seems to perform well with approx. 30+ mpg and a clean exhaust with no tell tale blue oil smoke. Pulling power may be slightly down as it seems to fall off quickly against head winds or uphill gradients, when running constant changing up and down with overdrive even on the level.

Could you please suggest a possible cause and remedy for the above.

I would suspect excessive bore or piston and ring wear causing excessive crankcase pressure blowing out the oil. This would also explain the lack of power.

A rebore and pistons would appear to be the answer. The engine can be rebored without taking it out of the vehicle. A detailed internal inspection of the engine would confirm this.

We recently paid a well known converter of diesel engines to Land Rovers and Range Rovers a handsome sum to convert our 1960 Land Rover to a Rover V8. He better remain nameless as "abortion" would be a better word to describe the conversion.

The exhaust system was a mangle of welded and leaking pipes which stuck out almost at ground level, which we replaced with the super Jake Wright Conversion. The fuel system had three different sized pipes all leaking and one set to self destruct on the hot manifold as were two of the water pipes to the rear heater.

The remote oil filter pipes rubbed against the sharp edge of the battery bracket. Our own H. D. Battery was replaced with a small torque start, there being insufficient room under the bonnet. The remains of the air filter system was fitted facing the rear bulkhead. Apparently to avoid a too-short lead from coil to distributor.

A high capacity electric pump flooded the engine and no return for excess fuel was fitted. A Kenlow fan was fitted but the engine overheated, we again solved this by fitting the thinner series III radiator and a special American aluminium fan from Jake Wright. The old thick rad did not give enough clearance for a normal or any other type of fan. It cost us over £125 to have the carb tuned and correct needle jets fitted.

We had to replace arcing plug leads. The wiring was a plumber's nightmare, and we had to replace too thin starter leads. There were other minor problems which I will not bore you with.

It now runs quite well apart from two problems on which we would like your advice. On tickover, oil pressure gauge drops to zero and green warning light flickers. I do not however think the engine when running has any wear problems to cause low oil pressure and have some vague thought that when a remote oil filter is fitted high up you have to remove the pressure release valve or do something or other.

The second problem is that where the engine joins the Series IIa gearbox there is a half moon gap, this could cause serious problems of mud and dirt if we have to wade across mud to pick up some dismounted horse rider. I think the bulge of the flywheel would prevent us making a straight plate to cover this aperture. Somebody did mention a Range Rover Auto, or something, might cover this aperture. Do you have a part number for something that we might adapt.

The most likely cause for the low oil pressure is a sticking pressure relief valve. It is situated in the oil filter head and should be removed, cleaned and any burrs polished off with 1200 grit wet and dry.

Refit with new spring. If this doesn't cure the problem, then it may be the remote filter connected the wrong way round or too thin pipes to the remote filter. Failing these it could just be a "tired" engine.

The part you require is FRC 2859. It should fit straight on.

My 1982 Land Rover Stage 1 V8 station wagon performs well at low speeds, but when pulling in the gears or at higher speeds, lacks the power I would have thought the V8 should deliver.

The Stage 1 V8 was fitted with restrictors behind the carbs to "strangle" the power down to comply with type approval regulations. If you remove the carbs you will see behind them the restrictor "plug" with three smaller holes in it. Sometimes they pull out and sometimes they need breaking up with a chisel (after removing the manifold). This will give you quite a

Re-boring in-situ.

Perkins four pot

considerable increase in power, so watch the roadholding!

I have recently bought a 1980 LWB Stage One V8. The problem is its lack of power. I got it principally to tow my trailer about but it can hardly get itself along. It runs out of steam at 60, which takes an awful long time to achieve and the first hint of a hill its down the box to third. I have been told these engines were derated to 90hp by a plate under the carbs. Can this be removed simply, or are there other modifications to be made.

The engine has been on an electronic diagnosis machine (like a Sun tester) and everything was shown to be set just about right.

The restrictors fitted to the Stage One V8 are easily removed by removing the carbs and pulling the restrictor from the manifold. They are in fact aluminium discs with three holes about 3/8". diameter in each one and are held in by an expanding steel clip. Select a suitable diameter tap and tap a thread with a smear of grease on the top to collect swarf, fit a long bolt and lever out with a pry bar. Extremely obstinate ones may be split into three large bits with a small chisel and pulled out. Clean the debris out with a vacuum cleaner. A piece of 1/2" hose taped onto the suction pipe will reach most places in the manifold.

I own an ex-military 1958 2¼ litre petrol 24 volt SWB of which the bottom end is worn out. I am in two minds whether to change the engine or repair it. If I am to change it I feel that I might as well put a larger engine in it, could you please advise me what would be the best petrol engine and would I have to convert it to 12 volt; which I don't really want to do.

Rebuild your original engine or replace with 2¼ as the fitting of a larger engine requires extensive modification to the rest of the vehicle i.e. brakes, gear ratios, tyres etc. If you fit a larger engine you will have to convert to 12v.

I want to install a Perkins 4203 engine in my ex-army Land Rover which is currently fitted with a 4 cylinder petrol engine.

Are the 4 cylinder engine mounts suitable to take a Perkins engine without chassis welding and will this engine give me more torque for towing than the present engine.

On conversions that I have seen the fan seems to be too close to the radiator. Is it possible to fit an electric fan in front of the radiator and would this give sufficient cooling for pulling a heavy load up very long and steep gradients?

Finally do you know anyone who undertakes this conversion work.

Yes the chassis mounts will take the 4203. The engine will give a lot more torque but you will need an overdrive or the top speed will only be in the mid forties.

An electric fan will cool the engine but fit a thermostatically controlled switch. A mechanical fan is more reliable for long slogs as it can move more cooling air.

To find someone able to do the work look in the LRO ads.

We recently purchased a 1983 Land Rover County 110 2.25 petrol. On our recent annual holiday we towed our boat to Yugoslavia. Whilst we were very pleased with its towing capabilities and cruising speed were were extremely disappointed with its ability to pull up the slightest incline.

Is there any way of improving

this. It has been suggested that perhaps a Fairey Overdrive would give more flexibility between gears.

Another suggestion has been that the only solution would be the fitting of a Rover SDI engine which I understand would also give much better mpg. The latter does however seem rather drastic.

The 2.25 engine usually performs well in the 110. Check that the throttle linkage is giving full movement on both chokes of the carb. As it is a progressive twin choke a small loss of movement such as a carpet tucked under the pedal can mean a big power loss.

Check also that the vacuum advance unit is working on the distributor (with the distributor cap off suck on the small pipe from the carb and watch for movement on the base plate where the points are fitted).

An overdrive unit will not fit your five speed gearbox.

The fitting of the V8 SDI unit is not as straight forward as it appears.

This requires a V8 110 Bell housing and first motion shaft fitting to the gearbox, a major strip down, wiring changes, new chassis mounts, hoses, exhaust, etc. and so is probably not worth the effort.

I have recently purchased an ex-MOD, FFR 24V 1974 Series III, 2.25 petrol soft top. I have now converted to 12V and put a 2.5 BMC diesel into it. The problem is that, although it pulls like a train, I can't get any more than 35 mph out of it, comfortably, that is. Is there anything I can do to improve this other than fitting an overdrive? I am thinking of things like transfer ratios or perhaps 900 × 16 tyres will fit 7.50 × 16 wheel rims. I don't want to change the diffs.

The 900 × 16 tyres will only fit forward control rims. As the rear diff ratio is hard to alter and the different diff ratios do not make a large difference, your only option is an overdrive.

I want to restore my 1967 LWB and hope to end up with a functional, economic vehicle. I want a galvanised chassis but I also want a diesel engine of about 3 litres capacity. As I am not planning to spend a lot on the engine I need something I can perhaps restore myself. What do you suggest. Is stripping and restoring the diffs a reasonable proposition given the number of special tools required, or would I be better off replacing them as a whole?

The Perkins 4203 diesel of 3.3 litres would probably be your best choice. It will fit the LR chassis without modification. The cost is relatively low (£300-£500) and including overhaul and adaptor kit should not cost over £1,000 plus the cost of an overdrive needed to achieve a realistic cruising speed.

Replace them as a whole. Secondhand units may be purchased for approx £50. As you intend to fit a larger engine a Salisbury rear axle as fitted to Series 3 LWB which is much stronger than your present axle, should be considered.

I am the proud owner of a Series III Lightweight. This is the third lightweight I have owned, but the first 24 volt one. How about an article on converting from 24v to 12v in some future issue. I was also thinking about dropping a Rover 3.5 into the vehicle. I have already fitted high ratio diffs but the engine seems powerless at about 60-65mph (no more acceleration) so the idea of a 3.5 crossed my mind. Is this a good idea or not, because I do some long distances at regular times.

Throttle opening

As most FFR (24v) vehicles have many surplus wires and relays fitted when in 'civvy' use I have found that the easiest and cheapest way of converting to 12v is to buy a 12v wiring loom for a civvy L/R, 12v alternator and bracket, battery carrier, distributor, coil, starter motor, flasher unit and of course bulbs and headlamps. Remove the resistor from the heater fan and wiper motors and rewire to the civvy pattern. This way you can now have a third front seat and not have any potentially dangerous surplus wiring. If you like originality then a simple change of distributor and leads allows normal spark plugs to be used with a 24v system.

To convert to a V8 there is a lot more than "dropping" a 3.5 engine into the vehicle.

To create a safe and reliable vehicle the brakes need uprating to LWB specification with a servo. The exhaust system needs fabricating properly and all fuel lines, water pipes and wiring needs to be properly engineered. If you are not a competent engineer I would recommend you did not attempt this. We have seen many disastrous conversions!

A normal 2¼ does not run out of steam at 60mph. Check that on full throttle the carb is actually on full throttle. 24v distributors do not have provision for a vacuum ignition timing advance only a mechanical system which is prone to failure. Also as the 24v plugs are very expensive these are seldom changed once out of the forces. A 'civvy' distributor and plugs should cure this. You do not comment on the general state of the engine possibly a decoke, piston rings and cylinder head skim (up to 65 thousandsths of an inch) which will give you the performance and reliability you require.

I am extremely confused by the popularity of the Rover V8 3.5 litre engine especially as it is so thirsty. Is it not obviously wiser to install a 2.8 litre Ford power unit (as advertised in LRO). After all, it does provide 135 bhp as opposed to only 114 bhp and yet gives better fuel economy.

Most Rover V8 engines people fit to LR are 165 or 155 bhp car engines. They are eligible for ARC events such as RTV Trials

Military oil-cooler.

and to "dyed in the wool" enthusiasts Ford is a four letter word!

I should be grateful if you could answer a few technical queries for me.

Was the large oil cooler used on the Series IIA military Land Rovers a success. The flexible oil return pipe attached via a banjo union to the side of the sump looks rather vulnerable to impact from rocks etc. Does this arrangement have problematical history? I am considering installing a second hand one I purchased on my 1981 SWB 2.25, 5-bearing petrol engine. I find when operating the vehicle in the bush at slow speeds, in air temperatures in excess of 35°C that the water temperature gauge is in the red though the thermostat has been removed and fan belt and tension are in good order. The radiator has not yet boiled over. The engine appears to be in good order having recently had an upper cylinder overhaul and new valves and has a very modest oil consumption. Does the Land Rover petrol engine have a reputation for inadequate cooling when operated in tropical climates? I brought the vehicle with me from the UK. Are there other measures I could take to improve its cooling.

Should the ignition timing be changed for use of the vehicle at higher altitudes? The Repair Operation manual indicates that the carburettor jets should be changed but no mention is made of the ignition timing. I currently set the ignition timing of my 8:1 compression ratio engine, using 90 octane fuel (Note: An ethanol

blend is used here) to Top Dead Centre. The elevation in Harare is in excess of 1500m.

The military type oil cooler gives no problems in use. Fit the whole system including oil temp gauge, multiblade fan and oil pressure relief valve. The timing should not be altered for altitude variations.

I want to improve the performance on my 1973 Range Rover by installing a US V8. What would be best — a small block Chevy, Ford or Chrysler? What about a 6.2 litre GM diesel? Which engine do you prefer (fuel costs aren't the problem). It is only legal to raise the power by 20 per cent because of Swiss car laws. Is it possible to improve off road driving and what are the biggest possible tyres?

Your RR already has a US V8 engine, a Buick. As you are only allowed to increase the power by 20% this can easily be achieved by changing the camshaft, carburettors (for a four barrelled Holley and Offenhouser manifold as fuel costs are not a problem!) and fitting tubular extractor manifolds to the exhaust. Large power increases are not sensible on a seventeen year old vehicle without major overhaul, steering, suspension etc.

Raising the suspension will not improve off road driving but will be detrimental to on road driving. It is possible to get to most places with a standard vehicle suspension or heavy duty suspension.

I have a 1982 109 Safari. The vehicle was originally a petrol but before I bought it the engine was replaced with a Gold Seal factory rebuilt diesel unit. Now I have a problem with the water sender unit which started when the pre-heater switch broke and started to burn. I replaced this

Diesel kits

but then noticed that the fuel and temperature gauges were not working. A Land Rover mechanic replaced the stabiliser unit behind the dash — the fuel gauge worked again but not the temperature gauge.

The mechanic this time replaced the water temperature sender unit on the engine block — it has a black top with a long stem. After running the engine for a few miles, the gauge is up to the red.

Another Land Rover main agent told me I need part number GTR III — it has a short stem and a white top. However, this makes no difference. The Haynes manual says the sender unit should be a beige colour on later models.

Can you help?

The part you require is 560794 (Genuine Parts). This is equivalent to GTRIII which is a Unipart number. As you have fitted two of these to no avail I would try the gauge itself. As your Land Rover has been fitted with a non-original switch to work the glow plugs and this has caught fire, there may have been a short circuit which damaged the voltage stabiliser and temperature sender unit and has probably damaged the gauge itself. The colour of the sender unit is not significant.

I recently bought a Series IIA ex-military Land Rover with the intention of completely rebuilding it over the next few years ending up with a vehicle that will last for years to come. I have been in touch with a firm that will supply me with a new galvanised chasis which will accept any engine and gearbox conversion I choose. Unfortunately, I cannot get many details on the best and most cost

effective diesel conversion. I have been quoted costs ranging from £2,000 to £5,000 and I would like to know if you can give me any advice on which of the more common Ford, BMC, Perkins diesel engines can be obtained from scrappers, reconditioned and fitted.

Also, can you give me any information on what, if anything, can be done to the standard gearbox other than fitting overdrive to improve its performance. My goal is to make a vehicle that I can comfortably and economically travel anywhere in, so will the Ninety/One Ten suspension fit into a Series III without a great deal of work?

There are many kits available for fitting alternative diesel engines to Land Rovers. Personally I think that a Land Rover 2.25 litre with a proper rebuild, including pump drive gear, takes a lot of beating. BMC 2.2, 2.5, 3.4 and 3.8 litre engines will fit as will Perkins 4.203 (3.3 litre). Ford York 4-cylinder plus others from Toyota, Nissan and Mazda can also be fitted as can the VM 2.4 turbo from the Rover SDI.

The strongest gearbox is the late Series II main box with a Series III transfer box (no second gear syncro and large bearings in transfer gears and layshaft).

Fitting higher gear diffs will improve the top speed of the slow revving engine. These are available from the Range Rover (3.45:1) or the P5 and P4 range of Rover cars (3.54:1 and 3.9:1).

Don't forget the back axle as most conversions have a voracious appetite for half shafts and a LWB Salisbury axle is a good idea.

Finally, Ninety/One Ten suspension will not be a practical conversion for a Series II or Series III vehicle.

I am thinking of swapping the

2.6 litre petrol engine in my 1969 IIa LWB Safari for a Perkins 4203 diesel. Could you tell me please:
1) Is the 4203 direct or indirect injection?
2) Where do I connect brake servo at engine end?
3) Is my 2.6 radiator big enough for the diesel?
4) Will brakes or suspension need uprating?
5) How many filters needed on the fuel line?

1) The 4.023 can be direct or indirect injection depending on the original engine application.
2) You connect the brake servo to the exhauster pump fitted to the front of the engine.
3) Your radiator, if in good condition, is perfect for the diesel.
4) The brakes and suspension as fitted to the 2.6 are fine.
5) One fuel filter and water trap are sufficient on the fuel system unless operating the vehicle in a very dirty environment where two would be required.

I have a 1984 Range Rover minus engine and gearbox. Is it possible to fit a diesel engine and an auto gearbox without being too expensive?
The cheaper type engines as fitted to RR such as Perkins 4203 and 4236, Ford York, etc. are not suitable with automatic gearboxes. If you need an auto box then the only options are the bigger high reving (and expensive) engines such as the VM 3.6 six cyl or the Nissan 3.5 four cyl.

I am the proud owner of a 1988 Land Rover 2.5 Turbo Diesel. I do my own servicing which has so far been fairly straightforward. However, on the last service I had to check the tappets — after removing the rocker cover the only way I could turn the engine over was to put the car in gear and push it backwards. By the time I got to the last rocker I had been out of the garage, round the block three times, back up the drive and home in time for tea! Is there any way I can turn the engine over without moving the vehicle.

Another item on this service was to remove, check, clean and adjust the injectors. Having read the LR Workshop Manual this task involves the use of special tools. I have adopted the policy of leaving well alone until they play up and then I will replace them with a set of exchange recons. What are your views on this?

Changing the subject slightly the brake pads and linings are showing no signs of any wear after over 24,000 miles. Is this normal or am I just a good driver? Also the tyres (Michelin 205/16 M&S) are less than half worn. My theory is that living in Lincolnshire most roads consist of hundred yard straights followed by a 90° bend to the right then another hundred yard straight and a 90° bend to the left — just to go round somebody's field — in fact if it wasn't for the drainage ditches you could travel in straight lines — assuming you have a Land Rover that is. Anyway when I approach a thirty mile an hour bend I usually go round at sixty thus going round on two wheels — halving the wear on the tyres. Do you think this is a good idea and do you think I could get a reduction on my Road Tax Fund Licence as 50 per cent of my

A five into a six

journeys are made on two wheels?

How many tins of paint would it take to change the colour of my LR?

Oops I must go now there is a policeman at the door — I wonder what he wants?

Disconnect the large multi plug on the wiring loom on the bulkhead. Pull the wire off the injector pump shut off solenoid as a safety measure and touch the starter solenoid wire (white with a red tracer) to a live feed (brown) on the engine side of the multi plug (check it is out of first gear first). An opened split pin is ideal for the job. With practice the engine can be flicked over to the required position.

Fuel injection systems should be left alone unless you have the specialist equipment and knowledge.

This is not unusual we know of one set on a 90 at 36,000 miles from new.

Three litres of two pack acrylic paint but use an air fed facemask as it contains cyanide.

Perhaps he thinks you only have a motorcycle driving licence!

I am the very proud owner of a Series IIA 2.25 LWB station wagon. I recently purchased what I believed, at the time to be a Perkins 4203 diesel engine together with the appropriate conversion kit. I checked the engine number with Perkins (whom I might add were extremely pleasant and helpful) who later found it to be the 4236, rated at 82 bhp.

The engine has done a genuine 25,000 miles so if possible I would like to make use of it. Therefore could you please tell me if it is feasible to fit this engine and will it prove to be too powerful for the IIA gearbox and overdrive. I have already fitted a

Salisbury axle to the vehicle.

The Perkins 4 (no of cylinders) 236 (size in cub inches) will fit into a LR but in a four cylinder such as yours space is limited and it is a tight fit. The six cylinder with the extra room in the engine bay allows the engine to fit more easily. The 189 lbf ft torque as compared to the 103 lbf ft of its original engine will certainly find any weakness in the transmission, the S2A gearbox will handle it better than an S3.

I am hoping to buy a 4-5 year old Ninety diesel. Is it possible to fit an after market turbo to this engine.

The turbo is not just a bolt-on "goodie" for a normally aspirated engine. The turbo engine has uprated valve gear, bearings, fuel pump and manifolding as well as improved cooling and lubrication systems. I would not expect the normal 2.5 engine fitted with an after market turbo to have the same longevity as the factory built turbo diesel engine.

The Turbo Ninety has been out since October 1986 and is available on the secondhand market, so I would go for one of those. If you do buy a Turbo Landy then check its service history as neglected oil changes in early life will show up later on.

I wonder if you could comment on the possibility of putting a Land Rover 5 bearing diesel engine into my 6 cylinder 109 inch chassis.

It is quite possible to put a 4 cylinder engine into your 6 cylinder Land Rover. The gearbox bell housing needs changing for a 4 cylinder version and the engine mountings must be cut off the chassis and moved backwards 6 inches. Use a 4 cylinder exhaust system and cut 6 inches from the front pipe. Use the 6 cylinder clutch. Throttle linkage can be adapted from 4 cylinder cable, fuel pipes need modifying and the electric fuel pump removed. Water pipes can be lengthened

Pre-production Land Rover number 8, owned by the author.

Series One, 86 inch wheelbase with canvas tilt.

Series One, truck cab pick up, 107 inch wheelbase.

Series II 109 inch wheelbase pick up with threequarter canvas tilt.

Series II 88inch wheelbase hardtop owned by the secretary of The Series II club.

Series IIB Forward Control.

Series III 88 inch wheelbase.

Airportable 88 inch wheelbase, known as the Lightweight.

101 Forward Control in Middle East military markings.

Coil sprung Ninety seven seater station wagon.

Defender 90 Hardtop Tdi.

One Ten on the Camel Trophy.

Two door Range Rover.

Range Rover Vogue — four doors and a spoiler.

Range Rover Vogue SE — the ultimate in luxury.

Discovery V8i 5-door.

or use One Ten pipes cut to suit.

Actually this makes quite a good conversion.

I have a Ninety Turbo Diesel. When it is worked hard it has the very nasty habit of blowing the engine oil filler cap/breather off. I also find that the diesel tank fitted is far too small, giving a very low range of around 240 miles without refuelling. Do you know of an auxiliary fuel tank kit for the Ninety?

It sounds as if your engine may have glazed bores and too much crank case pressure if the cap is blowing off. I suggest you have a compression check. I do not know of an auxiliary tank for a Ninety. Indeed, I have the same problem as yourself.

I'm a newcomer to Land Rovers and recently bought a 1975 Series III 88 inch. Chassis number is 90111387A and engine number 90174036B. Help! How do I tell the compression ratio and therefore which spark plugs to use?

The 901 in the engine number signifies it is a 2.25 litre, 8:1 compression ratio and three main bearing unit.

I have recently purchased a 1973 Land Rover FC Series IIB fire tender. Unfortunately the engine is beyond repair and requires a replacement. I have been told by fellow enthusiasts that the original 2.6 petrol engine was a very thirsty unit and they suggest that I should install either a diesel unit or a V6 petrol. What do you think?

I have found that the best engine in the IIB FC is the 3 litre straight six engine from the P5 Rover car. This has all the same dimensions as the 2.6 engine, fits easily and gives good fuel economy — we get 18 to 20 mpg from one we are running at present.

The Land Rover 2.25 diesel seems under-powered in an F.C. particularly one which is heavy such as a fire tender. There are diesel engines from Perkins which will fit — these are the 4.203 and 4.236 with suitable adaptors. It is not possible to fit an overdrive to an FC unless you replace the gearbox with a normal control gearbox — top speed is restricted to approximately 45 mph.

The Rover V8 will fit with an adapter, as will the Ford V6, but I feel the straight six, 3 litre Rover engine, which has lots of torque, is an ideal unit in these vehicles. It also looks like an original engine if you wish to preserve originality.

Could you recommend an alternative petrol engine to replace a 2.25 litre engine in a Series IIA long wheelbase. I want to retain the present engine's performance but increase the miles per gallon. The vehicle is already fitted with overdrive and free wheeling hubs.

The Rover V8 engine, whilst being more powerful, is also more fuel efficient than the 2.25 litre unit. With the correct gearing and a gentle right foot, figures of up to 25 mpg are possible. Alternatively, a more fuel efficient carb fitted with your present engine may help. Try a Weber or SU.

My 1976 Series III diesel SWB is losing engine oil through the engine breather cap mounted on top of the rocker box. Could the reason for this loss be caused simply by a poorly fitting breather cap and 'O' ring seal, or does it point to more serious matters? What remedy do you suggest?

Saharan hotspots

Try sealing the cap with a small amount of silicone sealer before replacing in the rocker box. A new rubber 'O' ring does not always cure the leak.

Questions, Questions, Questions about the V8.
a. Were all single valve spring heads of the SDI later type (with large valves and better porting)?
b. Are there two types, left and right handed rockers and how can you tell the castings apart?
c. If a pair of 8.5:1 heads were skimmed by 15 thou, by how much would the compression be altered?
d. What year did the SDI type engine become fitted in the Range Rover and from what engine number?
e. Was an engine fitted with the later SDI heads and a short early type pump?
f. As there are two types of crank rod assemblies, is it possible to swap complete assemblies between blocks containing different types (ie are the blocks different)?
g. What difference would fitting an HC car type vacuum advance and balance weights to a LC Range Rover engine running on four star petrol and re-timed make?
h. I am running a four speed Range Rover box which was perfectly good until I changed the oil. Now it baulks on first and second, especially from third to second. Could I improve it by running the gearbox on TQF instead of GTX oil?

a. Yes, the heads using the long reach spark plugs are better ported and valved than the earlier heads. Counting the valve springs can be misleading as single springs may be fitted to earlier heads.

substituted for each other.
c. The increase would be minimal.
d. The SDI engine has never been fitted to production Range Rovers, but an improved RR engine including some features found in the SDI engine was fitted in 1981. The numbers vary depending on the country the vehicle was destined for.
e. No.
f. The crankshafts are different depending on the type of rear oil seal (rope type or rubber lip seal) and cannot be swapped without machining.
g. The engine would not run as well as the distributor advance curve is wrong for this RR camshaft and heavy flywheel combination.
h. This is a worn box and someone has disguised its faults by running on Hypoid gear oil.

We recently purchased a SWB III diesel to drive across the Sahara. No. 4 heater plug kept breaking and inspection of the hot spots showed that No. 4 was loose. Our (supposedly reputable) garage recommended that all the hot spots should be replaced and the head skimmed. This was done and almost immediately we noticed increased engine noise. The garage dismissed this and unfortunately so did we. 3000 miles and much oil later, fortunately near a town on the Route du Hoggar, the engine seized up. Two hot spots had come loose, damaging pistons and the block. Good buy (sic!) one Land Rover! Another garage has since told us that they would never carry out a hot spot replacement on a diesel Land Rover engine and that a new cylinder head is the only

solution. Please could you confirm this?

ıt is perfectly possible to replace the hot spots in a Land Rover cylinder head. On a used cylinder head it is usual to 'pin' the hot spots in before skimming and replacing the head. This stops them working loose as yours have done and subsequently ruining the engine.

I am thinking of buying a SWB Land Rover but am unsure which engine to have fitted for both performance and ecomony. I have heard that the 2.25 LR diesel engine is very unreliable but the 2.5 BMC diesel is a good unit. Most of my driving is on tarmac with some beach work whilst on hols launching my boat.

The LR 2.25 diesel is a very reliable unit if looked after and not abused and will last many miles.

The same may be said of the BMC

engine but parts (service items or for disasters) are much more readily available for the LR unit. My preference is for the LR engine.

My wife and I are planning an extended trip to North Africa in our 1986 Range Rover Turbo D which has 50,000 miles on the clock. We need to ensure that the power plant and drive train are as reliable as possible. How does the reliability of the standard VM diesel compare with other installations and are there any specific problem areas that we need to focus on.

The VM 2.4 turbo has a good reliability record and will normally cover well in excess of 100 thousand miles. Being an intercooled unit the engine runs cooler than a non intercooled turbocharged diesel as the air fed into the engine is at a lower temperature and so the engine cooling

VM 2.4 turbo diesel in a Range Rover.

system does not have to dispose of as much waste heat.

A routine change of engine "consumables': water hoses, fan and pas belts and all filters and throttle cable together with a full service on the rest of the vehicle should see the RR fit for your trip.

I own a 1976 6 cylinder 2.6 109 which, despite a recent "head job" and six new exhaust valves is still rather gutless and thirsty. I recall in an earlier LRO article that a 3 litre version of this engine was made and is a good conversion. Is this engine available and is it a worthwhile conversion in terms of increased power and better fuel consumption? If so, is it compatible with the 2.6 in terms of gearbox, engine mountings and ancillaries? Would the head of my 2.6, recently overhauled, fit the 3 litre?

Yes it is available. Yes it is a worthwhile conversion. Yes it is compatible with the 2.6 engine (it shares the same cylinder block) and yes your head will fit. The Mark 1 engine has the same head. The Mark 2 engine however is fitted with a much improved Weslake head which is best left on. Try Exchange and Mart, magazine small ads or the P5 Rover Club.

I have a Series III 2.25 diesel and would like an engine that will give me better performance but maintain economy. In your last issue you recommend a Nissan TD27. Alternatively, what about the Land Rover 2.5 litre turbo?

The Land Rover 2.5 either turbo or normally aspirated engine will fit your Series 3 with little modification. Just use the S3 engine mounts and clutch plate and modified 110 exhaust system. Phone 0272

701314 for details and stockists of the TD27 engine.

(I have absolutely no connection with Nissan but have found them to be excellent replacement engines in Land Rovers and Range Rovers).

Can the 2.6 litre engine from 1980 to 1987 Rover cars be fitted to my IIA LWB?

The 2300 and 2600 engines as fitted to the SDI cars '76 to '87 did not have the best reliability record and will not easily fit a Land Rover. If you like 6 cylinders fit a P5 3 litre engine.

I would like to convert my early model One Ten V8 4 speed to diesel. As I cannot afford a new diesel engine I am considering an old slogger Perkins 4.236. I assume the standard radiator and exhaust will do, but will I have to raise the gearing? Would you advise turbo or non-turbo?

The 4.236 will fit using the Range Rover type fitting kit. Use the transfer gears as fitted to the post '81 Range Rover 4 speed gearbox. The turbo unit is more powerful than the normally aspirated unit. It is also quieter! Make sure the engine is from a road vehicle and not from an industrial application as the fuel injector pump will need recalibrating for road use.

My wife and I saved over a number of years to get enough money together for a decent Land Rover. We achieved our goal 18 months ago when we finally bought a 2.5 diesel Ninety, low mileage and in very good condition. Although over the moon with it generally, I am disappointed with the lack of power in the naturally aspirated diesel engine. It is not because I am comparing it with petrols either, as I have driven diesels for 12 years or so. What would you suggest?

The normally aspirated Ninety diesel should perform better than the 2.25 Series III vehicles you have run before. Check that the timing is correct. One tooth out on the rubber timing belt makes a lot of difference. Check also that you are getting full movement on the injector pump when you push the throttle to the floor.

I am rebuilding a 1965 LWB Safari IIA and have opted to exchange the 2.25 for a V8. I have a 3500S 10.5:1 engine but should I use a Range Rover or SDI flywheel and what about the clutch/pressure plate assembly?

The Range Rover flywheel is heavier than the SDI flywheel and is not best suited to the 3500S engine. Use clutch plate FRC2297 and cover 571228. These will fit the SDI (or P6 3500S which is the same) flywheel without modification.

I have a SWB IIA petrol and some time ago a slightly higher lift cam was fitted from Piper and the timing was set to Piper's spec. However, the vehicle seems slower to move off. Now that I have also fitted 750 × 16 SAT tyres the vehicle is very sluggish. I am told the solution would be to change the diffs, but to which ones? I read about 3.54, 4.3 and 3.9, what do they mean, which is best and will it solve the problem or should I just change back to a standard cam?

Changing the diffs for higher geared ones would only compound your problem. Change the camshaft for a standard one as, without increasing the compression ratio, improving the breathing and other engine modifications, the high lift cam alone has reduced the engine's performance and reduced its torque.

The ratio numbers quoted mean the number of turns of the propellor shaft for one turn of the road wheel. The standard SII Land Rover has 4.7:1 diffs which mean

the pinion shaft of the differential turns 4.7 times (as does the prop shaft, hand brake drum etc.) for one revolution of a road wheel.

I am the owner of a 1977 109 Hard Top which is fitted with the original 2.25 litre petrol engine. It is fitted with a reconditioned overdrive and freewheeling hubs. This is now starting to burn oil and I am thinking of changing the engine to a diesel.

The reasons for a diesel engine would be greater fuel economy and cheaper fuel as well as greater torque. I would like the same amount of performance as from the petrol engine therefore I do not really want a Land Rover Diesel. Also as I am planning to travel around Europe and perhaps further afield, I would like an engine that is easy to work on and obtain spares for.

I am also planning to fit a new galvanised bulkhead and I am wondering if it would be best to fit this before or after the new engine is installed?

The Nissan TD27 naturally aspirated engine would fit the requirements. As this is a new (as opposed to a rebuilt second hand) engine it should last a long time and parts are available worldwide. No modification is required to the bulkhead so it would be possible to replace either before or after the engine replacement.

We hear many reports that the Land Rover 2.5 litre turbo diesel engine is underpowered, drinks oil and needs constant servicing. Can the new Discovery 200 TDi turbo diesel engine be fitted into a 110 as a replacement engine?

The 200 TDi will fit the 90/110 and will fit straight up to the gearbox. The 200 TDi is now fitted to the Defender range and

Hot or cold?

it looks as if the old Land Rover 2.5 litre unit will be dropped. This may be to facilitate assembly, as at present there are three 2.5 litre turbo diesel engines in use — the VM in the Range Rover, the 200 TDi in the Discovery and the 2.5 in the Defender — or it may be that the Land Rover unit is not as reliable as other Land Rovers have been and Land Rover Ltd have realised this.

I recently changed my 1971 Range Rover for a 26,000 miles, high compression engine, 1984 model. I achieved around 18 mpg in the early model but can only manage 15 mpg in the '84. I have retarded the ignition to run on lead-free, but find that the vehicle is an uncertain starter and will not achieve 50 mph in third gear up an incline. It has been suggested to me that the vehicle will go faster if the Pulsair system is removed. A recent test showed compression ranging from 170 psi to 150 psi. Do you have any suggestions?

The ignition does not need to be retarded on your carburettor engine to run on lead free. Retime as original. The later Range Rover, although slightly higher geared than the old model and quite a lot heavier, should do more than 50 mph in third. Firstly check that, when your foot is flat to the floor on the accelerator pedal, the carb linkage is fully open. This is a common cause for sluggishness as is the failure of the vacuum advance and retard unit on the distributor. Premature camshaft wear, even at 26,000 miles, is not unknown and this will result in poor performance — often there will be no tell-tale noise as the hydraulic cam followers will take up the slack.

Removal of the Pulsair system will not significantly affect the performance or improve the mpg, so is best left alone. The compression figures, whilst not particularly low, suggest that it may be camshaft wear. The only real way to check this is to remove the inlet manifold and gasket and look at the camshaft lobes, comparing them with each other. If this is the case, then renewal will put the performance back on par.

Can you tell me the year of manufacture of my two and a quarter petrol engine number 90110300A. The previous owner tells me he thinks it came from a 1976 vehicle but the distributor and starter motor are dated 1972, 1971. However, the breathing system is of the sealed type, shown of pages ICO8 of the parts catalogue, which also states that these are used on engine suffix C to D.

The engine is from an early Series III of approximately 1971. The later breathing system could have been fitted or the engine fitted to a later vehicle. The starter and distributor are probably its originals.

Could you please help with two questions on a 1987 110 turbo diesel station wagon? 1. Should the valve clearances be adjusted hot or cold? 2. What is the road speed per 1000 rpm in the high range gears, particularly 4th and 5th?

1. Hot or cold.
2. 19.5 mph per 1000 rpm in fifth and 15.11 mph per 1000 rpm in fourth, assuming you are still on 7.50 × 16 tyres.

I am thinking of fitting a York six cylinder diesel with Bosch injection equipment and multiheater head to my 1986 110, non-turbo 2.5 diesel. I have had experience of this engine in a Range Rover, the only reliability problems being the cold starting, which the multiheater head should solve.

What are the drawbacks of this conversion in the 110?

This is not the best conversion, but fits well into the long engine bay. Use the Range Rover adaptor plate and SDI V8 bell housing. The use of the Bosch injector pump and having the head drilled for heater plugs is as good as this engine is going to be and, as such is a reasonable conversion, in relation to the cost. It is certainly more powerful than your original unit.

I have noticed that your opinion of the 2.5 litre turbo diesel engine is not good. Does this low opinion also apply to the normally aspirated 2.5 diesel? I was very seriously considering installing one of these engines in my 1967 IIA 109 truck cab. Now I'm having second thoughts. How about the 200 Tdi?

The turbocharging of the 2.5 engine seems to have found all the weaknesses of what is, after all, a 1957 design. The normally aspirated engine seems to be the limit, powerwise, for good reliability in this family of engines. Land Rover themselves seem to realise this as the Defender is now fitted with the 200 Tdi unit which seems a good engine. The non-turbo 2.5 diesel is as good an engine as any for your 11A, fits relatively easily and is a cost-effective conversion.

Can an exhaust brake be fitted to my 1989 Range Rover Vogue V8 auto as, on long declines it will gain enough momentum not only to rip the skin off a rice pudding, but take the table and chairs with it. I have been told that the torque converter locks up in low low. Is this so? If not, can I make this happen with some form of manual override switch?

An exhaust brake is only suitable for use on a diesel engine. The converter locks at road speeds of 40-44 mph by the use of a mechanical direct drive clutch. This will not work in first low, but there should be ample engine braking in this gear for steep descents unless one of the clutches in the gearbox is faulty. I would have the gearbox checked out as it seems to be at fault.

To achieve more power for towing in my two and a quarter petrol County, I want to fit a Rover 3.5 SD1 engine. Could you give you a brief resume of the work involved. Will any adaptor plates be necessary, any bell housing or flywheel alterations? Will there be any alterations needed to the bulkheads and footwells?

There are two ways of fitting a V8 to a 4-cylinder 90/110. The best way is to use a Range Rover or V8 Land Rover 5 speed gearbox. The Range Rover box needs to be the earlier type 1983-86, with the long gear lever. This will mate to your transfer box and if you use a Range Rover flywheel and 5 speed clutch, then the engine will be positioned in the normal Land Rover V8 position and a Land Rover V8 exhaust system will fit easily. The engine mounts on the engine will need re-working to fit the 4-cylinder chassis. There is no modification needed to the bulkhead.

The second way is to retain your gearbox, which has a shorter primary shaft than the V8 and fit the engine using the SD1 V8 bell housing or a V8 to Series III type adaptor plate. Both leave the engine some four inches further back in the chassis and need bulkhead modifications to the footwells to allow the back of the engine to clear. This route also means making up a suitable exhaust system and long radiator hoses and leaves a large gap between radiator and engine.

The first way is best but involves the extra expense of a gearbox. You will ultimately have a better vehicle however.

Is it possible and practicable to

Temperature gauge

convert the glowplug circuit on a Series III diesel from series to parallel wiring?

Rewiring from series to parallel will blow the plugs instantly. The 90/110 type plugs which are parallel wired will not fit your head, but I believe there is a type, new on the market, which will replace the old type and make them quicker to heat up and are parallel wired, so if one burns out the rest will start the engine.

I have used my 1957 SWB Series One for everyday use for over 20 years. It is still an excellent vehicle, capable of offering reliable motoring, even when asked to perform the unreasonable tasks required on a farm. I am very keen to retain its originality, but I would like to add a temperature gauge. I have been "caught out" in the past by fitting a radiator blind in winter, only to find the engine overheat in a mild spell or when working the Land Rover very hard. I have mounted a dual gauge on the dashboard using existing holes for the mounting screws. An oil gauge was easily fitted by inserting a "T-piece" in the oil pressure switch. I would like your advice as to the method and position of fitting the temperature sensor unit, bearing in mind that I want to retain originality. I am therefore trying to avoid cutting and carving as much as possible.

If you look at the thermostat housing on the nearside of your engine you will find next to the heater outlet a small boss cast onto the housing. Drill and tap to suit your sender unit. This is a "leftover" from the P3 car from where this type of engine was fitted and this is where the temp gauge sender is sited on vehicles used for stationary running such as fire engines.

I have a 1986 Range Rover which has covered 200,000 kms. A major overhaul of the mechanicals can't be too far away. I would like to replace the engine, clutch and transmission with a 3.9 unit. Could you advise me of any reputable wreckers who may have such a late model unit?

I'm not sure that he would like to be described as a "wrecker" but it may be worth contacting Peter Hobson at Windyridge, Donington on Bain, Lincolnshire (telephone: 0507 84737; fax: 0507 84393) as he dismantles fairly new vehicles.

The two and a quarter petrol engine on my Series III 1983 SWB has recently developed a noticeable "tapping" noise, but only when running cold or under load, e.g. towing or climbing a hill. If the throttle is eased back, the noise reduces considerably. The engine is standard apart from an unleaded head conversion some 5,000 miles ago: i.e. valve seats cut in, new valves, oil seals, guides etc. I have been told it could be an oil feed problem to the valve gear, but the pipe is clear. I am worried by suggestions of a) loose valve seat, b) sticking valve, c) small end bearing. The vehicle has done about 56,000.

The noise is probably pre-ignition, commonly called pinking. As you have an 8:1 compression engine (or slightly higher if the cylinder head has been skimmed) set the timing to 3 deg A T D C and the pinking should disappear. A loose valve seat usually falls out totally and damages the engine very quickly. A sticking valve stays stuck on a petrol engine and makes pops and bangs in the exhaust and a small end bearing is noisy under light load and goes quiet when going up hills, etc.

Will it fit?

A LOT OF the enquiries that we get are on the lines of "will a Series III such and such from a LWB fit my SWB Series II?" Or "can I fit a 5 speed gearbox to my '74 Range Rover?"

So here is an attempt to try to answer some of those questions by direct substitution or with a small amount of modification. After all, with time, money and patience, but no sense, it would be possible to fit a V12 Jaguar engine into an 80 inch!

Rover's policy of utilising parts which were already in production for a different model when building a new vehicle is particularly useful in places where spares are not as readily available. These lists are not exhaustive — if they were they would fill the entire book — but work on the principle of: if it looks as if it will fit, then it probably will.

Engines:

Petrol:
1600/2000 'F' head 4 cylinder
2600 'F' head SII and SIII 6 cyl (109″)
2250 OHV 3 bearing crank 4 cyl SII and SIII
2250 OHV 5 bearing crank 4 cyl SIII, 90, 110
2250 OHV 5 bearing crank 4 cyl 90, 110
3500 V8 SIII, 109, 90, 110 and Range Rover
Diesel:
2000 OHV 3 bearing crank 4 cyl
2250 OHV 3 bearing crank 4 cyl
2250 OHV 5 bearing crank 4 cyl
2500 OHV 5 bearing crank 4 cyl
2500 OHV 5 bearing crank 4 cyl Turbo

All the four cylinder engines are interchangeable. There are two types of bell housing stud patterns. F-head engines (overhead inlet and side exhaust valves) have one type and OHV engines the other. They all have common engine mounting bolt holes in the block and the depth from them to the back of the engine is common.

The six cylinder engine is 6 inches longer than a four cylinder and will not fit a 4 cylinder chassis without a great deal of modification, but a 6 cylinder, 3-litre car

Swapping engines

engine will fit a 6 cylinder Land Rover and made a good conversion. The V8 will not fit the 4 cylinder gearbox without an adaptor plate and suitably made engine mounts. The four cylinder diesel units will interchange with the four cylinder petrols with suitable pipework and wiring and throttle linkage. They will also fit the 6 cylinder 109 if the bell housing is changed and the engine mounts are moved back on the chassis.

Parts of the engines are interchangeable. For example, a Ninety cylinder head will fit, say, a 1972 SIII, but not *vice versa*.

In the 80 inch and 86 inch Land Rover, the engine bay is a bit too small to accommodate engines other than the 1600 and 2000 F-head. It later engines are fitted, the radiator needs moving forward to clear the fan blades.

When swapping engines, use the clutch assembly which is compatible with the gearbox you are using.

The V8 engines are all interchangeable with each other and the V8 car engines, but the front timing covers need changing for a Range Rover/Land Rover type when fitting car engines as the fan is too low otherwise.

Beware! The mixture of an SD1 engine, Range Rover flywheel and exhaust in a Range Rover does not give you the power that you might expect, so be careful when mixing engine components such as flywheels, camshafts, distributors and carbs from different engine applications.

Gearboxes

All Land Rover 4 speed gearboxes, with the exception of the V8 109 inch, are interchangeable. There are two types of bell housing stud pattern — the F-head type and the later 4 cylinder type which started with the 1958 2 litre diesel and is the same as the current Turbo diesel Defender and Discovery 200 TDi. Use one with the stud pattern to suit the engine or swap the bell housing.

There are early permanent four-wheel drive boxes with a free-wheel borrowed from the then current P3 car range (as were the main gearbox, brakes, diff, steering box and wheel, engine, etc.); two-wheel drive only boxes built for the 88 inch SI 2WD army contract; boxes with two synchro and boxes with three synchro and varying ratios in the transfer box, the lowest being in the One Ton and Forward Controls.

Two types of clutch system are used: SI and SII type with complicated external linkage and SIII type with simple arm within the bell housing. So if you use a box with the same bell housing stud pattern as your engine and use the clutch assembly to suit the box, they will all fit together.

Gearboxes (with common overall dimensions):

'F' head stud pattern
SI 4 speed 2 synchro constant 4WD
SI 4 speed 2 synchro part time 4WD
SI 4 speed 2 synchro 2WD only
SII 4 speed 2 synchro 6 cyl part time 4WD
SII 4 speed 2 synchro 6 cyl 1-ton part time 4WD
SIII 4 speed 3 synchro 6 cyl part time 4WD
OHV stud pattern
SII 4 speed 2 synchro 4 cyl part time 4WD
SII 4 speed 3 synchro 4 cyl part time 4WD
SIII 4 speed 3 synchro 4 cyl part time 4WD

Gearboxes (with common leading dimensions):

(Non-detachable transfer-box)
R/R 4 speed 4 synchro V8, 109, 110, permanent 4WD
(With detachable common shaped transfer boxes)
R/R 3 speed automatic permanent 4WD
R/R 4 speed automatic permanent 4WD
(With detachable bell housing)
R/R 5 speed short gearlever permanent 4WD

R/R 5 speed long gearlever permanent 4WD
90/110 5 speed part time 4WD 2.25 litre engines
90/110 5 speed permanent 4WD 2.5 litre engines and V8.

Internally, many of the components are common to the P3, P4 and P5 range of cars and across the Land Rover range of boxes, the external and internal components will swap. For example, the handbrake drum from a 1984 88 inch will fit a 1948 80 inch. The third fourth synchro hub from a P5 car will fit a SI, II and III box.

Range Rover, Ninety and One Ten boxes are all interchangeable as complete assemblies and the LT230T transfer box is also used on the 3 and 4 speed auto boxes (with different ratios). But things like hand brake levers and diff lock activators come in different places. The bolt holes through the chassis for the mounts are the same as are the leading dimensions of the boxes and the prop shaft positions.

The 5 speed bell housings all swap, so to fit a V8 into a 4 cylinder Ninety, just change the bell housing and first motion shaft.

The transfer ratios differ in different applications of what might appear to be the same thing: V8 Ninety — 1.222:1; V8 One Ten — 1.410:1 and V8 Range Rover — 1.192:1. This is to accommodate different tyre sizes and overall gearing. The 5 speed boxes will fit earlier 4 speed Range Rover if the 5 speed floor panel and gear levers are used.

So, to uprate an early Land Rover to 5 speed is quite possible as is fitting an auto box to a V8 One Ten, which is not a factory option.

Steering

80 inch steering boxes are unique and cannot be replaced by another without great modifications to the 80. 86 inch to 109 inch SI to SIII will all swap but there are two types of steering wheel splines. FC boxes have a longer column but the box internals are similar. PAS Range Rover boxes will fit early Range Rover manual if the PAS steering shaft is used. They will fit later manuals directly (82-ish onwards).

Ninety, One Ten and Range Rover boxes both power and later Range Rover manuals will swap with each other.

The latest type of drop arm with the replaceable ball joint will fit all power boxes and 82-ish onwards manual boxes, but not earlier manual boxes.

Axles

These are basic groups which can be subdivided further into groups, for example, extra reinforcing or different swivel bearings.

Non-Rover diffs

SII and SIII and FC ENV	front and rear leaf
SIII Salisbury	front and rear leaf
One Ten Salisbury	rear coil
Rover diffs	
SI narrow spring	front and rear leaf
SI wide spring	front and rear leaf
SII	front and rear leaf
SIII	front and rear leaf

R/R front and rear coil (imperial measurements)
R/R, 90, 110 (front) metric measurement coil

Rover diff ratios
'48 80" 4.88:1
'49-'58 SI 4.7:1
SII and SIII 4.7:1
V8 109 (front) 3.54:1
90, R/R, 110 (front) 3.54:1
Car diffs which will fit
Rover P4 (60-110) 4.7:1; 4.3:1 and 3.9:1
    P5 (3 litre) 4.3:1, 3.9:1
    P5B (3.5 litre) 3.54:1
P6 and SD1 diffs will not fit at all.

There are two axle types: leaf sprung and coil sprung. They are not interchangeable, but are within their group. Axles from other models will not fit 80 inch narrow springs unless the spring pads are modified. Forward control and LWB

Improving the ride

rear have spring pads set further apart than SWB. The 109 V8 has constant velocity joints within its hubs. SII and SIII have a wider axle than SI. The coil axles will interchange but have different braking systems on Ninety, One Ten and Range Rover. The One Ten also has a heavy duty Salisbury rear axle which will fit Range Rover and Ninety.

Many of the axle components will swap: a 1984, 88 inch swivel housing will fit a 1948, 80 inch. SWB brakes can be uprated by fitting LWB back plates, shoes and cylinders. SII hubs with the threaded type of stud can be replaced with the SIII type of splines.

All the Rover type diffs will interchange as long as you use the same ratio front and rear, but Range Rover front diffs need the flat base casting type to take the steering damper — these are also stronger diffs. Diffs from the P4 and P5 cars will also fit Land Rover and Range Rover axles.

As you can see, if you are in some far away place in your One Ten County and you damage the front diff, you can fit one from a dead Rangy or perhaps P5 coupé left behind by the diplomatic service in the 1960s. Or if your pride and joy 80 inch needs new swivel hubs, these are readily available.

Springs

All the leaf sprung Land Rovers use spring mounts on the chassis of common spacing. There are two spring widths: 1.75 inches and 2.5 inches — the narrow ones fitted to the rear of and some of the fronts of Series One 80 inch. Thus an air portable rear spring will fit a forward control and *vice versa* but they do, however, have differing numbers of leaves and different spring rates. That is for each incremental increase in loading, some springs will deflect less than others, or are "stiffer". So, obviously, the Forward Control with greater payload has stiffer springs than the air portable. However, in an **emergency**, they may be used until the correct spring is available.

Some substitutions, particularly on vehicles not used to carrying a lot of weight, make the ride better. For example, fitting LWB rear springs 279678 and 279679, which are soft springs with two big helper leaves, give a very good ride in a SWB which is used, say, for caravan towing.

Diesels have greater rate springs than their equivalent petrol models, as they are heavier vehicles. Increasing the spring rate of stiffness too much is not a good idea as it transmits forces into the chassis for which is was not designed and the vehicle is also uncomfortable to drive. Front leaf springs will not swap with rears.

Coil springs on Ninety, One Ten and Range Rover, are all the same diameter except for One Ten rear which are bigger. They will again swap in an emergency, but I feel they are best fitted with the manufacturer's specification for the vehicle, as changes often alter the handling for the worse. For example, if you mix springs from an unlevelled One Ten with those of a levelled One Ten, the ride and handling is poor. So stick to the design specification. Having said that, the manufacturer's part for one application may be the heavy duty part for another — NRC2119 is a standard Range Rover rear or heavy duty front spring.

Wheels

All Land Rovers and Range Rovers have the same number of studs and the same pitch circle diameter, so, potentially, all wheels are interchangeable. Earlier Land Rovers with the smaller wheel studs, were designed to carry most of the load on the large hole in the centre, so fitting Range Rover wheels, which carry the loading on the studs, is not on unless you change for the later SIII type hubs. Fitting Range Rover wheels on any SI to SIII Land Rover involves grinding of the drive flange to clear the wheels.

Competence required

The wheels come commonly in four widths — 5 inch SWB, 5.5 inch offset to the inside on LWB up to 1968-ish and 5.5 inch offset to the outside on the LWB, Ninety and One Ten. Six inch styled wheels are fitted to Ninety County and Range Rover. Alloy 6.5 inch wheels are fitted to the Range Rover Vogue. Vogue wheels should not be fitted to earlier Range Rovers unless the wheel studs are marked with a line on the end or are replaced with new ones. Range Rover steel wheels fit straight onto a Ninety or One Ten and look good, too. On any vehicle use four wheels all the same. All these wheels are 16 inch diameter. Some very wide wheels, 16 inch diameter were fitted to One Ten and Forward Control vehicles and 15 inch diameter were an option with sand tyres and were fitted to the Pink Panthers.

Tyres

Tyre sizes 600×16, 650×16, 700×16, 750×16 and 205×16 are all interchangeable if you use four of the same size and construction (radial or crossply). Fitting 205 radials to a SWB makes the ride better and the steering lighter. DO NOT fit tyres with a lower ply rating or lower speed rating than the manufacturer's vehicle specification as this is dangerous and illegal. Many people fit 750 crossplys to Range Rovers. This is illegal as they have a lower speed rating than the vehicle requires. All tyres should be fitted to wheels of appropriate width.

Bodywork

Most Land Rover body panels will fit if they look as if they will fit. For example, a One Ten station wagon rear door is the same as, with the exception of the additional hinge, a 1958 SII. An early One Ten side door will fit a SII or SII. If you can afford it and buy the locks as well, the latest Ninety/One Ten doors with wind-up windows will fit any SII, SIII or early One Ten.

A SII rear body will fit a SIII and so on.

SI 86 inch wings will fit an 80 inch. A SIII bonnet will fit a SII if you change the hinges. Ninety door mirrors and hinges will fit SII and SIII. So improving or updating an older model is quite easy.

LWB station wagon body sides will also fit SWB and make a good conversion.

Range Rover, with the exception of the doors, have totally interchangeable panels if you forget the latest bonnet with concealed hinges. Four-door body sides, doors and rear wings can be fitted to two-door vehicles.

As with Land Rovers, updating (and possibly a personal number plate) can be done to hide the true age of a Range Rover or to improve its appearance or replacement for accident or corrosion reasons with newer parts.

To summarise

When carrying out any substitutions, there are a number of aspects to consider.

Firstly safety. Are you fitting anything which may be potentially dangerous or impair the performance of items such as brakes, steering, etc.?

Secondly legality. Does the vehicle comply with the construction and use regulations applicable to its age? For example, if you fit SII wings and front panel with headlamps to a SIII, the lights would not meet legal requirements.

Thirdly, are you, or the person doing the work, competent enough to carry it out?

Armed with the right knowledge you can get out of many a difficult situation. Some years ago in some far flung corner of the British Empire (well, King's Lynn to be exact), I blew a head gasket on my Range Rover. A trip to the local agent found they had not got one in stock, but I managed to get one for a P6 car. As I only wanted the head and cam cover gaskets, these were identical.

I left the stores man wondering if it was him or me who was mad.

General

In an attempt to sharpen up the spongy brakes on my IIa, I am working on a process of elimination and the next venture was going to be flushing the system and changing the fluid. Having read about the silicone fluid supplied by Automex in JC's column I thought — I'll have some of that. Then in the June issue reader Roger James says he has used it and it caused the rubber seals to swell and advises we check that rubber seals are compatible with silicon fluid.

So I phone Automec to be told they hadn't heard of their product causing any such problem and as silicone is a lubricant, it would not have any adverse effect on rubber. So what do you think and who do we ask to find out if these rubber seals are compatible with silicone fluid?

Seals to original vehicle specification are compatible with silicone fluid. If poor quality replacements have been fitted they may react with the brake fluid. Before changing to silicone fluid you need to identify the problem on your vehicle as, unless your brake fluid is badly contaminated, the silicone fluid will not improve the sponginess.

What are the requirements and problems of changing my 109 V8 Safari from left hand to right hand drive. What do you think of fitting a Ford V6?
To convert to RHD you will basically need steering box, axle steering arm and dash pads and heater all available from any Series III. Brake pipes need modifying as does the wiring, gearlever and hand brake.

If you are not a very competent mechanic then entrust to someone who is or keep LHD.

On the V8 109 if you remove the carbs from the manifold you will find a restrictor plate with small holes to strangle the engine power to comply with EEC regulations for type approval. If you remove them and replace the carbs the vehicles will run a lot more efficiently and perform better all round. A V6 Ford would not be more efficient.

I am the proud owner of a One Ten County 1989 model. The front seats are comfortable enough but the next row, well. My daughters always moan. Is there any way of fitting two front seats there — I'm not worried about three across.

Yes, it is possible to fit two individual front seats in the middle or the middle seats from a 10 seater model give a lot more space (you have to fit shorter rear seats as well), but beware! If you reduce the seating capacity below 12 then you will be liable for 10% car tax and replaying the 15% VAT which as a business user you have reclaimed, as in the UK the 12 seater is classed as a commercial vehicle and the 10 seater is not.

Being something of a wimp and rather new to this macho vocation of sharing my life with our Series III SWB diesel Land Rover, I an anticipating a winter of discontent from my family. do I have to look out the old greatcoat, woolly hat, scarf and floves of my hippy days? Will I have to sew my children up in goose grease combinations? Will my wife have to resort to Damart longjohns? Or can I get the heater to work?

The SIII heater system works well in the SWB hard top vehicle. Check that the engine has a themostate fitted and working. The operating control is actually opening the water valve and allowing hot water to enter the heater matrix. The heater matrix on the SIII commonly blocks up if it is used with hard water so it may need cleaning out by a radiator specialist or

replacing as flushing with cleaning chemicals is not very effective. Lastly as the heater requires the fan to be blowing air from the n/s wing is the fan actually working?

For many years I have experience severe rain leakage through the canvas tilt on my Series III. I once made the mistake of coating another vehicle's tilt with polyurethane paint but the result was that it hung in tatters within a year as it became brittle. Can you recommend a course of action?

The only way to reproof a tilt is with a product specifically designed for the job. There are a large range of clear and coloured reproofing materials available from camping supply shops for tents and caravan awnings which are easy to apply and very effective. One such product is FABSIL which we have used on numerous occasions.

I have a 1971 IIA. Is there any way I can change the heater to increase the heat output? If not, is there any reason why I cannot put Tee pieces on the heater hoses to run another heater to the rear of the Land Rover thus running two heaters?

Yes it is possible to fit a heater in the rear of the vehicle. 'T' the hoses as suggested to run to a flat box heater as often found in older lorries such as the Leyland FG. The hoses can be run under the floor and clipped to the chassis.

I am currently 'aspiring' to buy a second-hand 110 Diesel or Turbo. However, over the months I have been looking I have become increasing frustrated over the issue of VAT. As I have a fairly tight budget I am looking to buy at around £6,000 to £7,500. However, at this price the addition of VAT is a hefty

The dreaded VAT

extra. **Whilst I have a reasonable understanding of the application of VAT to Land Rovers I am very unclear as to the use of VAT for second hand vehicles. Sometimes it applies and sometimes it appears not to apply. My frustration came to a head when I read an advert in a well known weekly which was for an attractive 1948 Series One the price of which has VAT added! How can this be? Surely anything manufactured before the implementation of the dreaded Value Added can not suddenly be VAT applicable? Who is the better off, the dealer, the government, it certainly is not the poor old Land Rover enthusiast who is not VAT registered. When I buy I pay it however when I sell I lose it. Can you help us to a better understanding?**

Land Rovers fall into two catagories with respect to VAT in the UK.

"Car type vehicles"

These include Range Rover, Discovery, 88 and 90 station wagons and 109 and 110 TEN SEATER station wagons. When purchased new, these are subject to 10% car tax plus 15% VAT, none of which is reclaimable by VAT-registered or non registered people. When sold later in life, they are not subject to tax again but a dealer is subject to paying 15/115ths of his profit. This again is unreclaimable.

"Commercial type vehicles"

These include 90 and 88 and ALL other shortwheelbase, 110 and 109 van and pickup bodied vehicles as well as 110 and 109 TWELVE SEATER station wagons. These attract 15% VAT when new which is reclaimable by a registered person and is recharged on resale price. This would again be reclaimable by a registered person. If at any point it is bought by a non-registered by a registered person. If at

any point it is bought by a non-registered person the VAT is not recoverable, but must be added on again if the vehicle is sold at some point in the future by a registered person.

Thus if a VAT registered person or company sells a commercial type (even a 1948 80") then they HAVE to charge the tax.

I want to rebuild my 107, 10 seater, 5 door 1957 station wagon, but I do not have a safari hard top. I have called several dealers and dumps in Holland and England but they all told me it's hard to find a hard top for these vehicles. Do you or any LRO reader, know where I can find the right hard top?

The roof for a 107 station wagon is rare in Britain. It is also unique, so a later top cannot be used as it is six inches narrower than the Series One. It is possible to cut a more readily available 86/88 inch Series One roof and fit a new piece of aluminium to the middle to make up the difference, but this is not really a perfect solution.

I own a 1984 Hi Capacity Pick Up which, on the whole, I am extremely pleased with apart from a couple of areas. The rear bar which protects the back of the cab is hardly a substantial piece of engineering and is too flimsy to tie anything to. The four speed gearbox seems to be very high geared. What is the cheapest way of lowering the gearing?

Safety Devices — 0638 661421 — will provide you with a suitable bar or manufacture you one to your specification. Your 110 is high geared because the gearbox has been replaced with a Range Rover unit at some point. This has higher geared transfer ratios than the 110 and, with its 750 tyres, makes the vehicle too high geared. Replace the transfer gears with 110 gears and it should return to normal.

I have a Turner drum winch (ex-MOD 1964) which is powered from the starting handle dog. Can this be fitted to a 90 County diesel?

I am sorry to say the winch will not fit. The 90 has a cross member at the front between the chassis rails which gets in the way. The only winches which will fit are either electrically or hydraulically powered. There is no provision for a front mounted mechanical winch on the 90/110.

I have a 1985 110 CSW. I would like to place the indicator on the right hand side of the steering column. Can this be done?

Remove the column shroud and slaken the clamping screw which holds the switch assembly to the column. Turn the switches round and tighten the screw. Replace the shroud but leave the screw out of the center of the lower panel as its locating point is now missing.

I own a 1989 2.5 turbo diesel 90 CSW. It has done just 3000 miles and the gearbox is very stiff when changing up from second to third gear, but not when changing down from fourth to third. Do you think it will loosen up in time? I am loathe to take it back to SMAC where I bought it new, as they seem to do more harm than good whenever it goes back there.

It is common for the gearchange to be stiff, but after 3000 miles I would have expected the "newness" to have bedded in. There is probably a problem with the syncromesh on 3rd gear and in view of the age, mileage and warranty, I suggest you have the vehicle repaired as this type of fault will not repair itself. If you are not happy with the service you are receiving from your dealer than contact the Customer Relations

Manager (Mr Jefferies) at Land Rover 021-722 2424 and make him aware of the situation.

I am about to acquire a C reg Range Rover EFi with a view to using it as my sleeping quarters on holiday. The two rear seats will have to go. Is removal straight forward, or should I leave it to the professionals?

Removal of the rear seat is easy. Fold foreward and remove the four bolts which go into the floor and carry the seat out. Remove the four bolts each side which bolt the backrest brackets to the body sides and you now have a two seater.

How can I obtain a set of Land Rover overalls? I have contacted several franchised dealers with no luck, being told that Land Rover only supply to their own service personnel.

Overalls are available to anyone from franchised dealers — not just for themselves. They are polyester/cotton in green with the Land Rover logo on the front from the Genuine Parts First Choice collection. Part number RTC 9642 for small; M, L, XL and XXL are available for the bigger sizes, all at £27.50 + VAT. If your dealer is still unable to help, ring Land Rover Parts Ltd on 021-781 6000 who will help.

I purchased a 90 turbo diesel 2.5 in October 1989. It was registered in August 87. Until six weeks ago I had first class service, then, suddenly, the crankshaft snapped. Could I claim anything from Land Rover?

It is unreasonable to think that a manufacturer would be responsible for a product more than three years after manufacture. BUT as the 2.5 turbo does not have the best reputation, it may be worth a try. At worst they can only say no! Write to: Mr S Jefferies, Manager — Customer Relations, Land Rover Ltd, Lode

Seatbelt fitting

Lane, Solihull, West Midlands B92 8NW, stating all the details like mileage, service history and so forth.

I need to replace the rear nearside body panel (rear wing) on my SWB IIA. Could you advise on the correct procedure please? I am not sure if this is spot welded on along the seat base structure to the rear.

The weld spots need to be drilled out and the easiest way is with a drill-like spot weld remover (see your local motor factor). With care, only the outer panel is drilled. The rear body capping is drilled off and the rear corner capping also. Pull the wing skin off and replace with the new. A certain amount of trimming may be required. Re-rivet as required. Counter sunk rivets may be used and then skimmed with a small amount of body filler to hide them.

I have belts and brackets for fitting safety belts to the middle row of seats in my One Ten. These are proper Land Rover parts but I cannot obtain fitting instructions. Can you advise me?

Secondly, I want a good ¾ length roof rack for my vehicle but can only locate rather basic utilitarian models. The April 89 issue of LRO shows what appears to be a suitable version on page 29, can you advise me where such a roof rack can be obtained?

The brackets should be MVC 1010/1 which are the shoulder anchorage brackets; 347884 (2 off) which are the wheel arch anchorage brackets and 348765 which are the anchor point tubes for the middle of the vehicle. You fit the lower brackets just inside the door shuts, the top ones behind the plastic trim behind the seat and the centre ones through the floor under the seats. If you do not feel competent enough to fit them then entrust the job to someone who is Instructions are not available but a

look at a vehicle fitted property with belts should clarify the fitting.

The roof rack was a test item and did not prove successful. Similar items are available from Land Rover Parts via your Land Rover dealer or contact Quest 80s on 0507 81401 or any of the many other advertisers in LRO.

Can you please give me some information on fitting a dual braking system complete with hydraulic or mechanical servo to my 1973 LHD 109 ex-military. A few years ago I saw a modification with two small hydraulic servos, one fitted to the front and one fitted to the rear brake pipes, ahead of the brake failure device. I was told at the time that this system had been adopted because it was impossible to fit a mechanical servo as fitted to the Series III without major surgery.

The most satisfactory servo is the mechanical servo which fits Series III and late Series II with no modification. Part number 569652 is the pedal assembly; the valve is 599443; master cylinder is NRC6096kkk and the servo itself is part number AEV1043. These are as fitted to the 109 V8.

I am thinking of purchasing a new Ninety Diesel Turbo hard top, is it possible to have it converted to take a full canvas tilt and who would undertake such a conversion?

The dealer supplying the vehicles, as the parts required are available from the factory. A new vehicle may be available built to special order to this specification but is not listed as a standard vehicle in this country.

We are buying a One Ten County and we were wondering if it is possible to fit central locking using Range Rover parts.

This is possible using RR or Rover SD1 solenoids but as a kit is not available a great deal of experimentation is required to get the system to work and it is virtually impossible to fit to rear door. I feel the time and skill required to engineer and reliable system would outweigh the benefits.

Could you tell me of any water proofing kit for my 1987 One Ten. Every time I go out in the rain or down a flooded road, the front carpets get soaked. I don't think the water is coming through the door seals.

Ingress of water into a 90/110 is a problem which Land Rover have not yet totally cured after seven years. Water comes through the roof seams through the windscreen frame and can even come around the rear vents and down the roof side rails to fall on the driver's knee when braking. In your case I suspect the water is coming through the seams on the bulkhead around the footwells. Thoroughly dry the inside of the seams and paint over with

automotive body and seam sealer (available in litre tins) followed by underseal. If the floor plates have ever been removed then the sealer around them may have been damaged and need replacing.

Can you please help me to find some waterproof seat covers. I have a Range Rover which has been customised with Vogue trim. The seat has one arm rest and has the safety belt coming out of the top of the seat. I have tried all the leading suppliers of seat covers and they are unable to help me. Perhaps you might even know where I might get some made.

Your local Land Rover Genuine Parts outlet should be able to supply you with tailored, easily fitted covers. The part number is RTC 8949 for a full set in bronze to fit the seats with single post head rests.

Six months ago I purchased a IIA. It has the usual seating

Range Rover waterproof seat cover.

Shut that door!

arrangement three seats across the front and bench seats along each side of the back. Is there a modification to allow forward facing rear seats. And what about seat belts?

John Craddock Ltd (05435 77207) are the only people I know who manufacture forward facing rear seats for a vehicle such as yours. It is possible to use a conventional lap and diagonal seat belt with these.

Can you advise the best source of information on the IIB Forward Control?

The instruction manual which covers the IIB FC is part number LSM 641M. The parts catalogue is part number 608218 and the workshop manual is part number 4611.

I have unsuccessfully been searching for a set of military rear bumpers. Do you have any ideas?

The bumpers you describe are readily available from military vehicles (see ads in LRO). However, they will only fit a military pattern rear cross member.

I had hoped to purchase high-ratio Salisbury diffs for a Series III to take back to Australia. Are these available? If so, where? If not, where could I purchase high-ratio Rover type diffs to fit a Series IIA. I had also hoped to find a power steering unit to fit a Series IIA or III. Does anyone make these?

The high-ratio diffs that you require, 3.54:1, were fitted to the Series III V8 (the complete axle will fit) or the crown wheel and pinion from the One Ten will fit your axle.

I have a 1972 Series III SWB petrol. This winter I hope to perform a major rebuild and, as part of this, I would like to modify the braking system. I feel

that there is no need to fit a servo or the brakes from the LWB, but I would like the safety of dual circuit brakes. Could you suggest a suitable master cylinder to fit in replacement of the original?

Unfortunately, due to the higher pedal pressures required, most twin circuit systems require a servo. Utilise a servo, pedal and master cylinder from the later 88 inch SIII.

I am delighted with my recently purchased 1985 Ninety truck cab, but for the door keeps. Both door posts have been previously dented and although the keeps are still in place, the doors, when fully open, touch the posts. Has anyone invented a modification.

My new Ninety suffers from the same problem! The modification we have done in the past to vehicles (particularly in windy areas) is to screw to the door edge and footwell a strip of seat belt webbing which, when taught, stops the door touching the door post. When fitting it, trap the webbing under two small strips of aluminium to stop the screws pulling through.

I own a 1983 One Ten County and two a large caravan. It would help a lot when reversing if the power steering was lighter. Can you tell me if anything can be done.

The power steering on your vehicles should allow the wheel to be turned easily by one hand. I suspect the steering is heavy because it is faulty. Check the PAS belt for tightness and that the filter is not blocked. Check that the Swivel housings are not seized on the swivel pins and that the steering box has not been over-adjusted. If nothing obvious is found then the pump needs testing to ensure it is delivering the correct pressure. Lastly, are the tyres inflated correctly?

I have a 1957 SWB Series One, chassis number 116700041, which has a two litre diesel engine which was factory fitted. Can you tell me if this Land Rover is one of the first to be factory fitted with a two litre diesel. I have had this Land Rover for 18 years and rebuilt the engine once about six years ago. I use it every day for work — do you suppose current models will last as long?

Yes, your Land Rover is one of the first right hand drive home market vehicles. Chassis numbering started 116700001, so yours is a very early diesel. Time with tell with 90s and 110s. They will last if looked after like your Series One. Corrosion is the main killer of Land Rovers and, as with human ailments, prevention is better than cure. So regular waxoiling and preventative maintenance, is the secret to long life and reliable service.

A simple problem. Rain. Despite renewing the door trim, the rain runs through the door tops of my 109. At first it was just the driver's door, but now the other side doors are starting to leak. I have added stick-on stuff and silicone sealer with no success. I now wear Drizabone which works, but my feet get wet and I don't like wearing wellies. Any ideas? Also, how easy is it to replace the window runners on the doors and rear body?

Leaks are relatively easy to fix if you can find their source. A garden hose is useful here to help. There are many places Land Rovers leak. If the leak is high up, then it is probably the roof to gutter joint which is sealed from new and, as the sealer ages, it allows water to enter the vehicle. Re-sealing with white mastic in the joint will stop water ingress at this point. The window runners are replaced by finding the

screws which hold the channel down and unscrewing them. This is usually easier said than done as they rust and are difficult to find. Re-fit new channel and re-drill and screw into frame. The rear channels are held in a similar way, but the shiny rail on which the window locks run needs removing as this holds the channel in as well.

I have the opportunity to buy a used Aero Winch Ltd, capstan winch, outwardly quite similar to the Fairey unit. It appears to function properly but is missing the engaging lever, shear pins and drive shift. Do you know of a source of parts?

Parts for the Fairey winch will fit as it is the same unit. They should be available through the normal parts network.

I like the Discovery, but it's a bit small. As no long wheelbase version is planned would it be possible to convert a standard Discovery into, say, a 110 inch wheelbase, putting in a couple of extra doors?

The idea is very possible, but would be better carried out on a factory produced four door (which should be available soon) as adding extra doors and pillars will increase the cost of conversion enormously.

I want to fit a V8 to my '67 SWB. What parts do I need to uprate the brakes? The bulkhead footwells are quite bad, is it practical to fit a new bulkhead bearing in mind the V8 conversion? Is it feasible to remove the bulkhead behind the front seats?

You will need to fit LWB brakes, master cylinder and servo. The footwells need cutting and rewelding for a V8, so it would be easier to repair yours at the same time as, if you buy a new bulkhead, it will need chopping and welding just the same. It is

Seeing the light

possible to remove the interior bulkhead but it supports the sides of the body and its removal weakens the structure. If the strength is replaced with a box section framework, then all is well. If not, the body will flex and the doors etc. will not fit properly.

I have a problem. People keep running into the back of my Range Rover with boring regularity. Thankfully only minor shunts so far and the tow bar has taken the impacts. I feel the need for some proections for the wings, but three tow bars would look silly. What would you suggest.

I suggest you check that your stop lights work when you press the brake pedal. If they do then a rear mounted bull bar (see adverts in LRO yellow pages) should limit the damage.

What type of headlamp do you consider best for the Series III? I replaced the sealed beam units in my 1971 IIA with halogen quad optic lamps. The improvements were a little disappointing and five years on, corrosion has eaten well into the relective surfaces.

Refitting the original sealed beam units has now improved matters!

The normal sealed beam 7" headlight unit is probably the best unit for the SIII Land Rover. The unit will not corrode and does not have the sharp beam pattern cut off of modern halogen lights. The light output is quite sufficient for the speeds the vehicles are capable of.

I am intrigued by the capstan winches fitted to the Range Rovers on the Darien Gap crossing. Can I fit one to my 101? I have been told they are not compatible with the V8 engine.

A capstan winch, part number RTC 8875, is available for Range Rovers and as such is compatible with the V8. With slight adjustment to the mechanism and cutting the bumper, it should fit (I haven't a 101 here to check). There is a side-mounted winch for the 101 which pulls either to the front or rear, but these are relatively uncommon.

The original camouflage paint on my ex-army 109 FFR is starting to look a little tatty andd is flaking off in places. I plan to repaint it but would like to keep it in its present colours. Where can I obtain similar coloured paints and what primer should I use on the places where bare metal is visible. Finally, where can I obtain a circuit diagram for the electrical system?

Use an etch primer to key the paint onto areas of bare aluminium. Camouflage paint is usually available from ex-military dealers (see ads in LRO). A wiring diagram is shown in the owners handbook for the three quarter ton 71-85, available from the LRO bookshop.

My father and I have owned a 1965 Series IIA for two years. We have virtually finished the mechanical work on it and the engine and chassis are in almost original condition. We are moving onto the exterior paintwork, but our job seems to be marred by the dull, ugly, stained look of the galvanised steel. Is there any simple and inexpensive solution to this problem?

There is no easy solution. The only real way is to remove the components and have them regalvanised. Thinned silver Hammerite is quite effective if applied carefully, but the real answer is regalvanising.

How old is your Rover?

A comprehensive listing of vehicle, chassis, engine, gearbox and axle numbers

Year and Model	Vehicle and Chassis Commencing Numbers	Engine Commencing Number	Gearbox Commencing Number	Front axle Commencing Number	Rear axle Commencing Number
1948-49					
L-R Basic Home R.H.D.	R860001 to 863000 and R866001				
L-R Basic Export L.H.D.	L86001 to 863000 and L866001				
Series I '80'					
L-R S.W. Home R.H.D.	R867001	860001	860001 R.H.D.	860001 R.H.D.	860001
L-R S.W. Export L.H.D.	L867001		L860001 L.H.D.	L860001 L.H.D.	
L-R Welder Home R.H.D.	R868001				
L-R Welder Export R.H.D.	R868001				
1950					
L-R Basic Home R.H.D.	R06100001				
L-R Basic Export L.H.D.	L06100001				
L-R Basic Export R.H.D.	R06100001				
Series I '80'					
L-R S.W. Home R.H.D.	R06200001	06100001 R.H.D.	06100001 R.H.D.	0610001 R.H.D.	06100001
L-R S.W. Export L.H.D.	L06200001	L06100001 L.H.D.	L06100001 L.H.D.	L06100001 L.H.D.	
L-R S.W. Export R.H.D.	R06200001				
L-R Welder Home R.H.D.	R06300001				
L-R Welder Export L.H.D.	L06300001				
L-R Welder Export R.H.D.	R06300001				
L-R C.K.D. L.H.D.	L06100001				
L-R C.K.D. R.H.D.	R06100001				
L-R 50 Prototype 2 litre	07100001	07100001	06100001	06100001	06100001
1951					
L-R Basic Home R.H.D.	16100001				
L-R Basic Export L.H.D.	16130001				
L-R Basic Export R.H.D.	16160001				
L-R S.W. Home R.H.D.	16200001				
Series I '80'					
L-R S.W. Export L.H.D.	16230001	16100001 R.H.D.	16100001 R.H.D.	16100001 R.H.D.	16100001
L-R S.W. Export R.H.D.	16260001	16130001 L.H.D.	16130001 L.H.D.	16130001 L.H.D.	
L-R Welder Home R.H.D.	16300001				
L-R Welder Export L.H.D.	16330001				
L-R Welder Export R.H.D.	16360001				
L-R C.K.D. L.H.D.	16630001				
L-R C.K.D. R.H.D.	16660001				

1952

Series I '80'

L-R Basic Home R.H.D.	26100001	26100001 R.H.D.	26100001 R.H.D.	26100001 R.H.D.	26100001
L-R Basice Export L.H.D.	26130001	26130001 L.H.D.	26130001 L.H.D.	26130001 L.H.D.	
L-R Basic Export R.H.D.	26160001				
L-R Welder Home R.H.D.	26300001				
L-R Welder Export L.H.D.	26330001				
L-R Welder Export R.H.D.	26360001				
L-R C.K.D. L.H.D.	26630001				
L-R C.K.D. R.H.D.	26660001				

1953

Series I '80'

L-R Basic Home R.H.D.	36100001	36100001 R.H.D.	36100001 R.H.D.	36100001 R.H.D.	36100001
L-R Basic Export L.H.D.	36130001	36130001 L.H.D.	36130001 L.H.D.	36130001 L.H.D.	
L-R Basic Export R.H.D.	36160001				
L-R Welder Home R.H.D.	36300001				
L-R Welder Export L.H.D.	36330001				
L-R Welder Export R.H.D.	36360001				
L-R C.K.D. L.H.D.	36630001				
L-R C.K.D. R.H.D.	36660001				

1954

Series I '86'

L-R Home R.H.D.	47100001	47100001 R.H.D.	47100001 R.H.D.	47100001 R.H.D.	47100001
L-R Export L.H.D.	47130001	47130001 L.H.D.	47130001 L.H.D.	47130001 L.H.D.	
L-R C.K.D. R.H.D.	47160001				
L-R C.K.D. L.H.D.	47130001				
	47660001				

Seris I '107'

L-R Home R.H.D.	47200001	47100001 R.H.D.	47100001 R.H.D.	47100001
L-R Export L.H.D.	47230001	47130001 L.H.D.	47130001 L.H.D. 10" brakes	10" brakes
L-R Export R.H.D.	47260001		47200001 R.H.D.	47200001
L-R C.K.D. R.H.D.	47760001		47230001 L.H.D. 11" brakes	11" brakes
L-R C.K.D. L.H.D.	47730001			

1955

Series I '86'

L-R Home R.H.D.	57100001, 57110001 and 170600001	57100001, 57110001 and 170600001 R.H.D.	57100001, 57110001 and 170600001 R.H.D.	57100001, 57110001 and 170600001
L-R Export L.H.D.	57130001, 57140001 and 173600001	57130001, 57140001 and 173600001 L.H.D	57130001, 57140001 and 173600001 L.H.D.	
L-R Export R.H.D.	57160001, 57170001 and 176600001			
L-R C.K.D. L.H.D.	57630001, 174600001			
L-R C.K.D. R.H.D.	57660001, 177600001			

Year and Model		Vehicle and Chassis Commencing Numbers	Engine Commencing Number	Gearbox Commencing Number	Front axle Commencing Number	Rear axle Commencing Number
L-R Home R.H.D.	Series I '107'	57200001, 57210001 and 270600001	57100001, 57110001 and 170600001 R.H.D.	57100001, 57110001 and 170600001 R.H.D.	57200001, 572100001 and 270600001 R.H.D.	57200001, 57210001 and 270600001
L-R Export L.H.D.		57230001, 57240001 and 273600001	57130001, 57140001 and 173600001 L.H.D.	57130001, 57140001 and 173600001 L.H.D.	57230001, 57240001 and 273600001 L.H.D.	
L-R Export R.H.D.		57260001, 57270001 and 27660001				
L-R C.K.D. L.H.D.		57730001, 274600001				
L-R C.K.D. R.H.D.		57760001, 277600001				
1956						
L-R Home R.H.D.	Series I '88'	111600001	170600001 R.H.D.	170600001 R.H.D.	170600001 R.H.D.	170600001
L-R Export R.H.D.		112600001	173600001 L.H.D.	173600001 L.H.D.	173600001 L.H.D.	
L-R C.K.D. R.H.D.		113600001				
L-R Export L.H.D.		114600001				
L-R C.K.D. L.H.D.		115600001				
L-R Home R.H.D.	Series I '109'	121600001	170600001 R.H.D.	170600001 R.H.D.	270600001 R.H.D.	27060001
L-R Export R.H.D.		122600001	173600001 L.H.D.	173600001 L.H.D.	273600001 L.H.D.	
L-R C.K.D. R.H.D.		123600001				
L-R Export L.H.D.		124600001				
L-R C.K.D. L.H.D.		125600001				
L-R S.W. Home R.H.D.	Series I '107' S.W.	87060001	170600001 R.H.D.	170600001 R.H.D.	270600001 R.H.D.	87060001
L-R S.W. Export L.H.D.		87360001	173600001 L.H.D.	173600001 L.H.D.	273600001 L.H.D.	
L-R S.W. Export R.H.D.		87660001				
L-R S.W. C.K.D. L.H.D.		874600001				
L-R S.W. C.K.D. R.H.D.		877600001				
1957						
L-R Home R.H.D.	Series I '88' Petrol	111700001	111700001 R.H.D.	111700001 R.H.D.	111700001 R.H.D.	111700001 Semi-floating
L-R Export R.H.D.		112700001	114700001 L.H.D.	114700001 L.H.D.	114700001 L.H.D.	111780001 Fully-floating
L-R C.K.D. R.H.D.		113700001				
L-R Export L.H.D.		114700001				
L-R C.K.D. L.H.D.		115700001				
L-R Home R.H.D.	Series I '88' Diesel	116700001	116700001 R.H.D.	116700001 R.H.D.	111700001 R.H.D.	111700001 Semi-floating
L-R Export R.H.D.		117700001	119700001 L.H.D.	119700001 L.H.D.	1147000071 L.H.D.	111780001 Fully-floating
L-R C.K.D. R.H.D.		118700001				
L-R Export L.H.D.		119700001				
L-R C.K.D. L.H.D.		120700001				

Series I '109' Petrol

L-R Home R.H.D.	121700001	111700001 R.H.D.	111700001 R.H.D.	121700001 R.H.D.	121700001
L-R Export R.H.D.	122700001				
L-R C.K.D. R.H.D.	123700001				
L-R Export L.H.D.	124700001	114700001 L.H.D.	114700001 L.H.D.	124700001 L.H.D.	
L-R C.K.D. L.H.D.	125700001				

Series I '109' Diesel

L-R Home R.H.D.	126700001	126700001 R.H.D.	111700001 R.H.D.	121700001 R.H.D.	121700001
L-R Export R.H.D.	127700001				
L-R C.K.D. R.H.D.	128700001				
L-R Export L.H.D.	12970001	129700001 L.H.D.	114700001 L.H.D.	124700001 L.H.D.	
L-R C.K.D. L.H.D.	13070001				

NOTE: The fifth digit of 1957 Land-Rover '88' rear axle number indicates a fully-floating axle.

Series I '107' S.W.

L-R S.W. Home R.H.D.	131700001	111700001 R.H.D.	121700001 R.H.D.	131700001
L-R S.W. Export R.H.D.	132700001			
L-R S.W. C.K.D.R.H.D.	133700001			
L-R S.W. Export L.H.D.	134700001	114700001 L.H.D.	124700001 L.H.D.	

1958 Series I

Series I '88' Petrol

L-R Home R.H.D.	111800001	111800001 R.H.D.	111800001 Semi-floating
L-R Export R.H.D.	112800001		
L-R C.K.D. R.H.D.	113800001		
L-R Export L.H.D.	114800001	114800001 L.H.D.	111880001 Fully-floating
L-R C.K.D. L.H.D.	115800001		

Series I '88' Diesel

L-R Home R.H.D.	116800001	116800001 R.H.D.	111800001 Semi-floating
L-R Export R.H.D.	117800001		
L-R C.K.D. R.H.D.	118800001		
L-R Export L.H.D.	119800001	119800001 L.H.D.	111880001 Fully-floating
L-R C.K.D.R.H.D.	120800001		

Series I '109' Petrol

L-R Home R.H.D.	121800001	111800001 R.H.D.	121800001
L-R Export R.H.D.	122800001		
L-R C.K.D. R.H.D.	123800001		
L-R Export L.H.D.	124800001	114800001 L.H.D.	
L-R C.K.D. L.H.D.	125800001		

Series I '109' Diesel

L-R Home R.H.D.	126800001	126800001 R.H.D.	121800001
L-R Export R.H.D.	127800001		
L-R C.K.D. R.H.D.	128800001		
L-R Export L.H.D.	129800001	129800001 L.H.D.	
L-R C.K.D. L.H.D.	130800001		

Year and Model	Vehicle and Chassis Commencing Numbers	Engine Commencing Number	Gearbox Commencing Number	Front axle Commencing Number	Rear axle Commencing Number
L-R S.W. Home R.H.D.	131800001	111800001 R.H.D.	111800001 R.H.D.	121800001 R.H.D.	131800001
L-R S.W. Export R.H.D.	132800001				
L-R S.W. C.K.D.R.H.D.	133800001				
L-R S.W. Export L.H.D.	134800001	114800001 L.H.D.	114800001 L.H.D.	124800001 L.H.D.	
L-R S.W. C.K.D. L.H.D.	135800001				

Series I '107' S.W.

NOTE: The fifth digit of the 1958 Land-Rover '88' rear axle number indicates fully-floating axle.

1958 Series II

Year and Model	Vehicle and Chassis Commencing Numbers	Engine Commencing Number	Gearbox Commencing Number	Front axle Commencing Number	Rear axle Commencing Number
Home R.H.D.	141800001	141800001	141800001	141800001 R.H.D.	141800001
Export R.H.D.	142800001				
C.K.D. R.H.D.	143800001				
Export L.H.D.	144800001		144800001 L.H.D.		
C.K.D. L.H.D.	145800001				
Series II 88 Petrol					
Home R.H.D.	146800001	146800001	146800001	141800001 R.H.D.	141800001
Export R.H.D.	147800001				
C.K.D. R.H.D.	148800001				
Export L.H.D.	149800001				
C.K.D. L.H.D.	150800001				
Series II 88 Diesel					
Home R.H.D.	151800001	151800001	151800001	151800001 R.H.D.	151800001
Export R.H.D.	152800001				
C.K.D. R.H.D.	153800001				
Export L.H.D.	154800001			154800001 L.H.D.	
C.K.D. L.H.D.	155800001				
Series II 109 Petrol					
Home R.H.D.	156800001	156800001	156800001	151800001 R.H.D.	151800001
Export R.H.D.	157800001				
C.K.D. R.H.D.	158800001			154800001 L.H.D.	
Export L.H.D.	159800001				
C.K.D. L.H.D.	160800001				
Series II 109 Diesel					

1959

Year and Model	Vehicle and Chassis Commencing Numbers	Engine Commencing Number	Gearbox Commencing Number	Front axle Commencing Number	Rear axle Commencing Number
Home R.H.D.	141900001	151900001	151900001	141900001 R.H.D.	141900001
Export R.H.D.	142900001				
C.K.D. R.H.D.	143900001				
Export L.H.D.	144900001			144900001 L.H.D.	
C.K.D. L.H.D.	145900001				
Series II 88 Petrol					

Series II 88 Diesel

Variant					
Home R.H.D.	146900001	146900001	146900001	146900001 R.H.D.	141900001
Export R.H.D.	147900001			144900001 L.H.D.	
C.K.D. R.H.D.	148900001				
Export L.H.D.	149900001				
C.K.D. L.H.D.	150900001				

Series II 109 Petrol

Variant					
Home R.H.D.	151900001	151900001	151900001	151900001 R.H.D.	151900001
Export R.H.D.	152900001			154900001 L.H.D.	
C.K.D. R.H.D.	153900001				
Export L.H.D.	154900001				
C.K.D. L.H.D.	155900001				

Series II 109 Diesel

Variant					
Home R.H.D.	156900001	156900001	156900001	151900001 R.H.D.	151900001
Export R.H.D.	157900001			154900001 L.H.D.	
C.K.D. R.H.D.	158900001				
Export L.H.D.	159900001				
C.K.D. L.H.D.	160900001				

Series II 109 Petrol Station Wagon

Variant					
S.W. Home R.H.D.	161900001	151900001	151900001	151900001 R.H.D.	151900001
S.W. Export R.H.D.	162900001			154900001 L.H.D.	
S.W. C.K.D. R.H.D.	163900001				
S.W. Export L.H.D.	164900001				
S.W. C.K.D. L.H.D.	165900001				

Series II 109 Diesel Station Wagon

Variant					
S.W. Home R.H.D.	166900001	156900001	156900001	151900001 R.H.D.	151900001
S.W. Export R.H.D.	167900001			154900001 L.H.D.	
S.W. C.K.D. R.H.D.	168900001				
S.W. Export L.H.D.	169900001				
S.W. C.K.D. L.H.D.	170900001				

1960

Series II 88 Petrol

Variant					
Home R.H.D.	141000001	151000001	151000001	1410000001 R.H.D.	141000001
Export R.H.D.	142000001			144000001 L.H.D.	
C.K.D. R.H.D.	143000001				
Export L.H.D.	144000001				
C.K.D. L.H.D.	145000001				

Series II 88 Diesel

Variant					
Home R.H.D.	146000001	146000001	146000001	141000001 R.H.D.	141000001
Export R.H.D.	147000001			144000001 L.H.D.	
C.K.D. R.H.D.	148000001				
Export L.H.D.	149000001				
C.K.D. L.H.D.	150000001				

Year and Model		Vehicle and Chassis Commencing Numbers	Engine Commencing Number	Gearbox Commencing Number	Front axle Commencing Number	Rear axle Commencing Number
Home R.H.D.	Series II	151000001	151000001	151000001	151000001 R.H.D.	151000001
Export R.H.D.	109	152000001			154000001 L.H.D.	
C.K.D. R.H.D.	Petrol	153000001				
Export L.H.D.		154000001				
C.K.D. L.H.D.		155000001				
Home R.H.D.	Series II	156000001	156000001	156000001	151000001 R.H.D.	151000001
Export R.H.D.	109	157000001			154000001 L.H.D.	
C.K.D. R.H.D.	Diesel	158000001				
Export L.H.D.		159000001				
C.K.D. L.H.D.		160000001				
S.W. Home R.H.D.	Series II	161000001	151000001	151000001	151000001 R.H.D.	151000001
S.W. Export R.H.D.	109	162000001			154000001 L.H.D.	
S.W. C.K.D. R.H.D.	Petrol	163000001				
S.W. Export L.H.D.	Station	164000001				
S.W. C.K.D. L.H.D.	Wagon	165000001				
S.W. Home R.H.D.	Series II	166000001	156000001	156000001	151000001 R.H.D.	151000001
S.W. Export R.H.D.	109	167000001			154000001 L.H.D.	
S.W. C.K.D. R.H.D.	Diesel	168000001				
S.W. Export L.H.D.	Station	169000001				
S.W. C.K.D. L.H.D.	Wagon	170000001				

1961

Year and Model		Vehicle and Chassis Commencing Numbers	Engine Commencing Number	Gearbox Commencing Number	Front axle Commencing Number	Rear axle Commencing Number
Home R.H.D.	Series II	141100001	151100001	151100001	141100001 R.H.D.	141100001
Export R.H.D.	88	142100001			144100001 L.H.D.	
C.K.D. R.H.D.	Petrol	143100001				
Export L.H.D.		144100001				
C.K.D. L.H.D.		145100001				
Home R.H.D.	Series II	146100001	146100001	146100001	141100001 R.H.D.	141100001
Export R.H.D.	88	147100001			144100001 L.H.D.	
C.K.D. R.H.D.	Diesel	148100001				
Export L.H.D.		149100001				
C.K.D. L.H.D.		150100001				

Series II 109 Petrol

Home R.H.D.	151100001	151100001	151100001	151100001 R.H.D.	151100001
Export R.H.D.	152100001			154100001 L.H.D.	
C.K.D. R.H.D.	153100001				
Export L.H.D.	154100001				
C.K.D. L.H.D.	155100001				

Series II 109 Diesel

Home R.H.D.	156100001	156100001	156100001	151100001 R.H.D.	151100001
Export R.H.D.	157100001			154100001 L.H.D.	
C.K.D. R.H.D.	158100001				
Export L.H.D.	159100001				
C.K.D. L.H.D.	160100001				

Series II 109 Petrol Station Wagon

S.W. Home R.H.D.	161100001	151100001	151100001	151100001 R.H.D.	151100001
S.W. Export R.H.D.	162100001			154100001 L.H.D.	
S.W. C.K.D. R.H.D.	163100001				
S.W. Export L.H.D.	164100001				
S.W. C.K.D. L.H.D.	165100001				

Series II 109 Diesel Station Wagon

S.W. Home R.H.D.	166100001	156100001	156100001	151100001 R.H.D.	151100001
S.W. Export R.H.D.	167100001			154100001 L.H.D.	
S.W. C.K.D. R.H.D.	168100001				
S.W. Export L.H.D.	169100001				
S.W. C.K.D. L.H.D.	170100001				

Land-Rover Series IIA 1961-1971

Series IIA 88 Petrol

Home R.H.D.	24100001a	25100001a	25100001a	24100001a R.H.D.	24100001a
Export R.H.D.	24200001a			24400001a L.H.D.	
C.K.D. R.H.D.	24300001a				
Export L.H.D.	24400001a				
C.K.D. L.H.D.	24500001a				

Series IIA 109 Petrol

Home R.H.D.	25100001a	25100001a	25100001a	25100001a R.H.D.	25100001a
Export R.H.D.	25200001a			25400001a L.H.D.	
C.K.D. R.H.D.	25300001a				
Export L.H.D.	25400001a				
C.K.D. L.H.D.	25500001a				

Series IIA 109 Petrol Station Wagon

Home R.H.D.	26100001a	25100001a	25100001a	25100001a R.H.D.	25100001a
Export R.H.D.	26200001a			25400001a L.H.D.	
C.K.D. R.H.D.	26300001a				
Export L.H.D.	26400001a				
C.K.D. L.H.D.	26500001a				

Year and Model		Vehicle and Chassis Commencing Numbers	Engine Commencing Number	Gearbox Commencing Number	Front axle Commencing Number	Rear axle Commencing Number 1960
Home R.H.D.	Series IIA	27100001a	27100001a	25100001a	24100001a R.H.D.	24100001a
Export R.H.D.	88 Diesel	27200001a			24400001a L.H.D.	
C.K.D. R.H.D.	2¼ Litre	27300001a				
Export L.H.D.		27400001a				
C.K.D. L.H.D.		27500001a				
Home R.H.D.	Series IIA	27600001a	27600001a to 27600880a; then in the range 27100001a	27600001a to 27600880a; then in the range 27100001a	25100001a R.H.D.	25100001a
Export R.H.D.	109 Diesel	27700001a			25400001a L.H.D.	
C.K.D. R.H.D.	2¼ Litre	27800001a				
Export L.H.D.		27900001a				
C.K.D. L.H.D.		2800001a				
Home R.H.D.	Series IIA	28100001a	27600001a to 27600880a; then in the range 27100001a	27600001a to 27600880a; then in the range 27100001a	25100001a R.H.D.	25100001a
Export R.H.D.	109 Diesel	28200001a			25400001a L.H.D.	
C.K.D. R.H.D.	2¼ Litre	28300001a				
Export L.H.D.	Station	28400001a				
C.K.D. L.H.D.	Wagon	28500001a				

SIIA PETROL MODELS, 6 CYLINDER 2.6 LITRE ENGINE

109 Series IIA

Home, RHStg 34500001D
Export, RHStg 34600001D
Export, RHStg, CKD 34700001D
Export, LHStg 34800001D
Export, LHStg, CKD 34900001D

Series IIA

Home, RHStg, 109 Station Wagon 35000001D
Export, RHStg, 109 Station Wagon 35100001D
Export, RHStg, CKD, 109 Station Wagon 35200001D
Export, LHStg, 109 Station Wagon 35300001D
Export, LHStg, CKD, 109 Station Wagon 35400001D

SERIES III LAND ROVER COMMENCING VEHICLE NUMBERS
UP TO OCTOBER 1979

2¼ LITRE PETROL MODELS

88
Home	90100001A
Export RH Stg	90200001A
Export CKD RH Stg	90300001A
Export LH Stg	90400001A
Export CKD LH Stg	90500001A

109
Home	91100001A
Export RH Stg	91200001A
Export CKD RH Stg	91300001A
Export LH Stg	91400001A
Export CKD LH Stg	91500001A

88 Station Wagon
Home	92100001A
Export RH Stg	92200001A
Export CKD RH Stg	92300001A
Export LH Stg	92400001A
Export CKD LH Stg	92500001A

109 Station Wagon
Home	93100001A
Export RH Stg	93200001A
Export CKD RH Stg	93300001A
Export LH Stg	93400001A
Export CKD LH Stg	93500001A

2¼ LITRE DIESEL MODELS

88
Home	90600001A
Export RH Stg	90700001A
Export CKD RH Stg	90800001A
Export LH Stg	90900001A
Export CKD LH Stg	91000001A

109
Home	91600001A
Export RH Stg	91700001A
Export CKD RH Stg	91800001A
Export LH Stg	91900001A
Export CKD LH Stg	92000001A

88 Station Wagon
Home	92600001A
Export RH Stg	92700001A
Export CKD RH Stg	92800001A
Export LH Stg	92900001A
Export CKD LH Stg	93000001A

109 Station Wagon
Home	93600001A
Export RH Stg	93700001A
Export CKD RH Stg	93800001A
Export LH Stg	93900001A
Export CKD LH Stg	94000001A

2.6 LITRE PETROL MODELS

109
Home	94100001A
Export RH Stg	94200001A
Export CKD RH Stg	94300001A
Export LH Stg	94400001A
Export CKD LH Stg	94500001A

109 Station Wagon
Home	94600001A
Export RH Stg	94700001A
Export CKD RH Stg	94800001A
Export LH Stg	94900001A
Export CKD LH Stg	95000001A

1 TON MODELS

109 2¼ Litre Petrol

Home	24600001A
Export RH Stg	24700001A
Export CKD RH Stg	24800001A
Export LH Stg	24900001A
Export CKD LH Stg	25000001A

109 2.6 Litre Petrol

Home	26600001A
Export RH Stg	26700001A
Export CKD RH Stg	26800001A
Export LH Stg	26900001A
Export CKD LH Stg	27000001A

2¼ LITRE PETROL MODELS

88

Home RH Stg	LBAAH1AA100001
Export RH Stg	LBAAH1AA100001
Export CKD RH Stg	LBAAH1AF500001
Export LH Stg	LBAAH2AA100001
Export CKD LH Stg	LBAAH2AF500001

88 Station Wagon

Home RH Stg	LBABH1AA100001
Export RH Stg	LBABH1AA100001
Export CKD RH Stg	LBABH1AF500001
Export LH Stg	LBABH2AA100001
Export CKD LH Stg	LBABH2AF500001

109

Home RH Stg	LBCAH1Aa100001
Export RH Stg	LBCAH1AA100001
Export CKD RH Stg	LBCAH1AF500001
Export LH Stg	LBCAH2AA100001
Export CKD LH Stg	LBCAH2AF500001

109 Station Wagon

Home RH Stg	LBCMH1AA100001
Export RH Stg	LBCMH1AA100001
Export CKD RH Stg	LBCMH1AF500001
Export LH Stg	LBCMH2AA100001
Export CKD LH Stg	LBCMH2AF500001

2¼ LITRE DIESEL MODELS

88

Home RH Stg	LBAAG1AA100001
Export RH Stg	LBAAG1AA100001
Export CKD RH Stg	LBAAG1AF500001
Export LH Stg	LBAAG2AA100001
Export CKD LH Stg	LBAAG2AF500001

88 Station Wagon

Home RH Stg	LBABG1AA100001
Export RH Stg	LBABG1AA100001
Export CKD RH Stg	LBABG1AF500001
Export LH Stg	LBABG2AA100001
Export CKD LH Stg	LBABG2AF500001

109

Home RH Stg	LBCAG1AA100001
Export RH Stg	LBCAG1AA100001
Export CKD RH Stg	LBCAG1AF500001
Export LH Stg	LBCAG2AA100001
Export CKD LH Stg	LBCAG2AF500001

109 Station Wagon

Home RH Stg	LBCMG1AA100001
Export RH Stg	LBCMG1AA100001
Export CKD RH Stg	LBCMG1AF500001
Export LH Stg	LBCMG2AA100001
Export CKD LH Stg	LBCMG2AF500001

2.6 LITRE PETROL

109

Home RH Stg	LBCAP1AA100001
Export RH Stg	LBCAP1AA100001
Export CKD RH Stg	LBCAP1AF500001
Export LH Stg	LBCAP2AA100001
Export CKD LH Stg	LBCAP2AF500001

109 Station Wagon

Home RH Stg	LBCMP1AA100001
Export RH Stg	LBCMP1AA100001
Export CKD RH Stg	LBCMP1AF500001
Export LH Stg	LBCMP2AA100001
Export CKD LH Stg	LBCMP2AF500001

1 TON MODELS

109 2¼ Litre Petrol

Home RH Stg	LBDAH1AA100001
Export RH Stg	LBDAH1AA100001
Export CKD RH Stg	LBDAH1AF500001
Export LH Stg	LBDAH2AA100001
Export CKD LH Stg	LBDAH2AF500001

109 2.6 Litre Petrol

Home RH Stg	LBDAP1AA100001
Export RH Stg	LBDAP1AA100001
Export CKD RH Stg	LBDAP1AF500001
Export LH Stg	LBDAP2AA100001
Export CKD LH Stg	LBDAP2AF500001

COMMENCING VEHICLE INDENTIFICATION NUMBERS 109 V8 LAND ROVER
VEHICLE 109 V8 STATION WAGON

VEHICLE 109 V8

Home RH Stg	LBCAV1AA100001
Export RH Stg	LBCAV1AA100001
CKD RH Stg	LBCAV1AF100001
Export LH Stg	LBCAV2AA100001
CKD LH Stg	LBCAV2AF100001

VEHICLE 109 V8 STATION WAGON

Home RH Stg	LBCMV1AA100001
Export RH Stg	LBCMV1AA100001
CKD RH Stg	LBCMV1AF100001
Export LH Stg	LBCMV2AA100001
CKD LH Stg	LBCMV2AF100001

GEARBOX

88100001

FRONT AXLE

88100001 RH Stg
88400001 LH Stg

REAR AXLE

Salisbury number

ENGINE

Non-Detoxed 10500001
Detoxed 11G00001

Australia 12G00001
Detoxed

L/R SII & SIII ENGINE Nos. & TYPES WITH COMPRESSION RATIOS

MODEL	ENGINE TYPE	ENGINE SERIAL NUMBERS
Series IIA/III	2.25 litre diesel (3 bearing)	27100001 A to J → 27600001 A to J →
Series IIA/III	2.25 litre diesel (3 bearing)	27100001K → 9060001 A to J →
Series IIA/III	2.25 litre petrol 7:1 C.R. (3 bearing)	25100001 → 25300001 → 9040001 →
Series IIA/III	2.25 litre petrol (8:1 C.R.) (3 bearing)	24100001 → 90100001 → 90200001 → 9030001 →
Series III	2.25 litre petrol (7:1 C.R.) (5 bearing)	36400001C →
Series III	2.25 diesel (5 bearing)	366. . .B 366. . .C
Series III	2.25 litre petrol (8:1 C.R.) (5 bearing)	36100001C →
Series III	2.6 litre petrol	34500001 → 94100001 →

SII & SIII GEARBOX TYPES & SERIAL Nos.

MODEL	GEARBOX TYPE	ENGINE TYPE	GEARBOX SERIAL NUMBERS
Series IIA	4 speed incl. transfer box	2.25 litre petrol & diesel →	(G) 24600001 A →
Series IIA	4 speed part synchro incl. transfer box	2.25 litre petrol & diesel	(G) 23800001 C to G → (G) 25100001 C to G → (G) 25200001 C to G → (G) 25400001 C to G → (G) 27600001 C to G → (G) 90100001 C to G →

Model	Engine	Gearbox	Numbers
Series IIA	2.25 litre petrol & diesel	4 speed full synchro incl. transfer box	(G) 23800001 H → (G) 25100001 H → (G) 25200001 H → (G) 25400001 H → (G) 27600001 H → (G) 90100001 H →
Series III	2.25 litre petrol & diesel	4 speed incl. transfer box	(G) 90100001 A → (G) 90200001 A → (G) 90300001 A →
Series III	2.25 litre petrol & diesel	4 speed incl. transfer box	(G) 24600001 B & C → (G) 90100001 B & C → (G) 90200001 B & C → (G) 90300001 B & C →
Series III	2.25 litre petrol & diesel	4 speed incl. transfer box	(G) 90100001 D → (G) 90200001 D → (G) 90300001 D →
Series III	2.6 litre petrol	4 speed incl. transfer box	(G) 26600001 A & B →
Series III	2.6 litre petrol	4 speed part synchro incl. transfer box	(G) 34300001 F →
Series III	2.6 litre petrol	4 speed full synchro incl. transfer box	(G) 94100001 A →
Series III	2.6 litre petrol	4 speed incl. transfer box	(G) 94100001 A & B →
Series III	3.5 litre petrol	4 speed incl. transfer box	(G) 88100001 A →

Model	Vehicle and Chassis Commencing Number	Engine Commencing Number	Gearbox Commencing Number	Front axle Commencing Number	Rear axle Commencing Number
2¼ LITRE PETROL					
Home R.H.Stg	28600001A				
Export R.H.Stg	28700001A				
Export R.H.Stg C.K.D.	28800001A	28600001A	28600001A	28600001A R.H. Stg	28600001A
Export L.H.Stg	28900001A			28900001A L.H.Stg	
Export L.H.Stg C.K.D.	29000001A				
2.6 LITRE PETROL					
Home R.H.Stg	30000001A				
Export R.H.Stg	30100001A			28600001A R.H.Stg	
Export R.H.Stg C.K.D.	30200001A	30000001A	30000001A		28600001A
Export L.H.Stg	30300001A			28900001A L.H.Stg	
Export L.H.Stg C.K.D.	30400001A				

Model	Vehicle and Chassis Commencing Number	Engine Commencing Number	Gearbox Commencing Number	Front axle Commencing Number	Rear axle Commencing Number
2¼ LITRE PETROL					
Home R.H.Stg	32500001A				
Export R.H.Stg	32600001A			32500001A R.H.Stg	
Export R.H.Stg C.K.D.	32700001A	32500001A	32500001A		32500001A
Export L.H.Stg	32800001A			32800001A L.H.Stg	
Export L.H.Stg C.K.D.	32900001A				
2.6 LITRE PETROL					
Home R.H.Stg	33000001A				
Export R.H.Stg	33100001A			32500001A R.H.Stg	
Export R.H.Stg C.K.D.	33200001A	33000001A	33000001A		32500001A
Export L.H.Stg	33300001A			32800001A L.H.Stg	
Export L.H.Stg C.K.D.	33400001A				
2¼ LITRE DIESEL					
Home R.H.Stg	33500001A				
Export R.H.Stg	33600001A			32500001A R.H.Stg	
Export R.H.Stg C.K.D.	33700001A	33500001A	32500001A		32500001A
Export L.H.Stg	33800001A			32800001A L.H.Stg	
Export L.H.Stg C.K.D.	33900001A				

Model	Vehicle and Chassis Commencing Number	Engine Commencing Number	Gearbox Commencing Number	Front axle Commencing Number	Rear axle Commencing Number
12 VOLT VEHICLES					
R.H.D.	95600001A	95600001A 12v	95600001A R.H.D.		
R.H.D.	95700001A				
C.K.D.	95800001A				
L.H.D.	95900001A			95900001A LHD	95600001A
C.K.D.	96000001A				
24 VOLT VEHICLES					
R.H.D.	96100001A	96100001A 24v	95600001A	95600001A RHD	
R.H.D.	96200001A				
C.K.D.	96300001A				
L.H.D.	96400001A			95900001A LHD	95600001A
C.K.D.	96500001A				

VEHICLE INDENTIFICATION NUMBERING LR90

Vin Code	Engine	Gearbox	Steering
REGULAR			
SALLDVAH7AA000001	2.25 Petrol	5 Speed	RH Stg
SALLDVAH8AA000001	2.25 Petrol	5 Speed	LH Stg
SALLDVAC7AA000001	2.5 Diesel	5 Speed	RH Stg
SALLDVAC8AA000001	2.5 Diesel	5 Speed	LH Stg
SALLDVAV7AA000001	3.5 Petrol	5 Speed	RH Stg
SALLDVAV8AA000001	3.5 Petrol	5 Speed	LH Stg
STATION WAGON			
SALLDVBH7AA000001	2.25 Petrol	5 Speed	RH Stg
SALLDVBH8AA000001	2.25 Petrol	5 Speed	LH Stg
SALLDVBC7AA000001	2.5 Diesel	5 Speed	RH Stg
SALLDVBC8AA000001	2.5 Diesel	5 Speed	LH Stg
SALLDVBV7AA000001	3.5 Petrol	5 Speed	RH Stg
SALLDVBV8AA000001	3.5 Petrol	5 Speed	LH Stg

Engines
10H00001A 2.25 Petrol 8:1 CR Non detoxed
11H00001A 2.25 Petrol 8:1 CR Detoxed
13H00001A 2.25 Petrol 7:1 CR Low Compression
12J00001C 2.5 Diesel
19J00001C Diesel Turbo
14G00001A 3.5 Litre V8 8.13:1 Non Detoxed
15G00001A 3.5 Litre V8 8.13:1 Detoxed

Gearbox
50A00001A 2.5 P & 2.5 D
13C0001A 3.5 V8

Transfer Box
12D00001A 2.5 P & 2.5 D

Front axle
21L00001A RHS
22L00001A LHS

Rear axle
22S0001A
23S00001A (Heavy Duty)

VEHICLE INDENTIFICATION NUMBERING LR110

Vin Code	Engine	Gearbox	Steering
HOOD/CAB/HARDTOP			
SALLDHAH7AA000001	2.25 Petrol	5 Speed	RH Stg
SALLDHAH7BA000001	2.25 Petrol	5 Speed	RH Stg
SALLDHAH8AA000001	2.25 Petrol	5 Speed	LH Stg
SALLDHAH8BA000001	2.25 Petrol	5 Speed	LH Stg
SALLDHAG7AA000001	2.25 Diesel	5 Speed	RH Stg
SALLDHAG8AA000001	2.25 Diesel	5 Speed	LH Stg
SALLDHAC7AA000001	2.5 Diesel	5 Speed	RH Stg
SALLDHAC7BA000001	2.5 Diesel	5 Speed	RH Stg
SALLDHAC8AA000001	2.5 Diesel	5 Speed	LH Stg
SALLDHAC8BA000001	2.5 Diesel	5 Speed	LH Stg
SALLDHAV1AA000001	3.5 Petrol	4 Speed	RH Stg
SALLDHAV1BA000001	3.5 Petrol	4 Speed	RH Stg
SALLDHAV7BA000001	3.5 Petrol	5 Speed	RH Stg
SALLDHAV2AA000001	3.5 Petrol	4 Speed	LH Stg
SALLDHAV2BA000001	3.5 Petrol	4 Speed	LH Stg
SALLDHAV8BA000001	3.5 Petrol	5 Speed	LH Stg
STATION WAGON			
SALLDHMH7AA000001	2.25 Petrol	5 Speed	RH Stg
SALLDHMH7BA000001	2.25 Petrol	5 Speed	RH Stg
SALLDHMH8AA000001	2.25 Petrol	5 Speed	LH Stg
SALLDHMH8BA000001	2.25 Petrol	5 Speed	LH Stg
SALLDHMG7AA000001	2.25 Diesel	5 Speed	RH Stg
SALLDHMG8AA000001	2.25 Diesel	5 Speed	LH Stg
SALLDHMC7AA000001	2.5 Diesel	5 Speed	RH Stg
SALLDHMC7BA000001	2.5 Diesel	5 Speed	RH Stg
SALLDHMC8AA000001	2.5 Diesel	5 Speed	LH Stg
SALLDHMC8BA000001	2.5 Diesel	5 Speed	LH Stg
SALLDHMV1AA000001	3.5 Diesel	4 Speed	RH Stg
SALLDHMV1BA000001	3.5 Petrol	4 Speed	RH Stg

VIN	Engine	Transmission	Steering
SALLDHMV7BA000001	3.5 Petrol	5 Speed	RH Stg
SALLDHMV2AA000001	3.5 Petrol	4 Speed	LH Stg
SALLDHMV2BA000001	3.5 Petrol	4 Speed	LH Stg
SALLDHMV8BA000001	3.5 Petrol	5 Speed	LH Stg

HIGH CAPACITY PICK-UP

VIN	Engine	Transmission	Steering
SALLDHHH7AA000001	2.25 Petrol	5 Speed	RH Stg
SALLDHHH7BA000001	2.25 Petrol	5 Speed	RH Stg
SALLDHHH7BA000001	2.25 Petrol	5 Speed	RH Stg
SALLDHHH8AB000001	2.25 Petrol	5 Speed	LH Stg
SALLDHHH8BA000001	2.25 Petrol	5 Speed	LH Stg
SALLDHHG7AA000001	2.25 Diesel	5 Speed	RH Stg
SALLDHHG8AA000001	2.25 Diesel	5 Speed	LH Stg
SALLDHHC7AA000001	2.5 Diesel	5 Speed	RH Stg
SALLDHHC7BA000001	2.5 Diesel	5 Speed	RH Stg
SALLDHHC8AA000001	2.5 Diesel	5 Speed	LH Stg
SALLDHHC8BA000001	2.5 Diesel	5 Speed	LH Stg
SALLDHHV1AA000001	3.5 Petrol	4 Speed	RH Stg
SALLDHHV1BA000001	3.5 Petrol	4 Speed	RH Stg
SALLDHHV7BA000001	3.5 Petrol	5 Speed	RH Stg
SALLDHHV2AA000001	3.5 Petrol	4 Speed	LH Stg
SALLDHHV2BA000001	3.5 Petrol	4 Speed	LH Stg
SALLDHHV8BA000001	3.5 Petrol	5 Speed	LH Stg

Note In some instances the 7th digit in the VIN CODE for the High-Capacity Pick-Up will read 'A' instead of 'H'

Engines	Gearbox	Transfer Box	Front axle	Rear axle
10H00001A 2.25 Petrol 8:1 CR Non detoxed	50A00001A 2.25 P&D	10D00001A 2.25P&D 2/4 WD	20L00001A RHS	21S00001A
11H00001A 2.25 Petrol 8:1 CR Detoxed	2.5 D	2.5D 2/4 WD	21L00001A LHS	
13H00001A 2.25 Petrol 7:1 CR Low Compression				
10J00001A 2.25 Diesel		12D00001A 2.25P&D Perm 4WD		
12J00001C 2.5 Diesel		2.5D Perm 4WD		
19J00001C 2.5 Diesel Turbo				
14G00001A 3.5 Litre V8 8.13:1 CR Non detoxed 13C00001A 3.5 Litre V8				
15G00001A 3.5 Litre V8 8.13:1 Cr Detoxed				

RANGE ROVERS
1970-1979

Vehicle Identification Numbers (VIN Nos)

VIN	Doors	Steering	Transmission	Compression
35500001A	2 Door	UK RH Stg	4 Speed	Low Compression
35600001A	2 Door	Export RH Stg	4 Speed	Low Compression
35800001A	2 Door	Export LH Stg	4 Speed	Low Compression

VIN Nos from October 1979 — June 1984

SALLHABV1AA000001	2 Door	RH Stg	4 Speed	Low Compression
SALLHABV2AA000001	2 Door	LH Stg	4 Speed	Low Compression
SALLHABE1AA000001	2 Door	RH Stg	4 Speed	High Compression
SALLHABE2AA000001	2 Door	LH Stg	4 Speed	High Compression
SALLHABV7AA000001	2 Door	RH Stg	5 Speed	Low Compression
SALLHABV8AA000001	2 Door	LH Stg	5 Speed	Low Compression
SALLHABE7AA000001	2 Door	RH Stg	5 Speed	High Compression
SALLHABE8AA000001	2 Door	LH Stg	5 Speed	High Compression
SALLHABV3AA000001	2 Door	RH Stg	Automatic	Low Compression
SALLHABV4AA000001	2'Door	LH Stg	Automatic	Low Compression
SALLHABE3AA000001	2 Door	RH Stg	Automatic	High Compression
SALLHABE4AA000001	2 Door	LH Stg	Automatic	High Compression

SALLHAMV1AA000001	4 Door	RH Stg	4 Speed	Low Compression
SALLHAMV2AA000001	4 Door	LH Stg	4 Speed	Low Compression
SALLHAME1AA000001	4 Door	RH Stg	4 Speed	High Compression
SALLHAME2AA000001	4 Door	LH Stg	4 Speed	High Compression
SALLHAMV7AA000001	4 Door	RH Stg	5 Speed	Low Compression
SALLHAMV8AA000001	4 Door	LH Stg	5 Speed	Low Compression
SALLHAME7AA000001	4 Door	RH Stg	5 Speed	High Compression
SALLHAME8AA000001	4 Door	LH Stg	5 Speed	High Compression
SALLHAMV3AA000001	4 Door	RH Stg	Automatic	Low Compression
SALLHAMV4AA000001	4 Door	LH Stg	Automatic	Low Compression
SALLHAME3AA000001	4 Door	RH Stg	Automatic	High Compression
SALLHAME4Aa000001	4 Door	LH Stg	Automatic	High Compression

Montiverdi 4 Door

SALLHARV1AA000001	4 Door	RH Stg	4 Speed	Low Compression
SALLHARV2AA000001	4 Door	LH Stg	4 Speed	Low Compression
SALLHARE1AA000001	4 Door	RH Stg	4 Speed	High Compression
SALLHARE2AA000001	4 Door	LH Stg	4 Speed	High Compression
SALLHARV7AA000001	4 Door	RH Stg	5 Speed	Low Compression
SALLHARV8AA000001	4 Door	LH Stg	5 Speed	Low Compression
SALLHARE7AA000001	4 Door	RH Stg	5 Speed	High Compression
SALLHARE8AA000001	4 Door	LH Stg	5 Speed	High Compression
SALLHARV3AA000001	4 Door	RH Stg	Automatic	Low Compression
SALLHARV4AA000001	4 Door	LH Stg	Automatic	Low Compression
SALLHARE3AA000001	4 Door	RH Stg	Automatic	High Compression
SALLHARE4AA000001	4 Door	LH Stg	Automatic	High Compression

RR VIN NOS. JUNE 84-86

SALLHABV7BA000001	2 Door	RH Stg	5 Speed	Low Compression

VIN	Door	Steering	Transmission	Compression
SALLHABV8BA000001	2 Door	LH Stg	5 Speed	High Compression
SALLHABE7BA000001	2 Door	RH Stg	5 Speed	Low Compression
SALLHABE8BA000001	2 Door	LH Stg	5 Speed	High Compression
SALLHABV3BA000001	2 Door	RH Stg	Automatic	Low Compression
SALLHABV4BA000001	2 Door	LH Stg	Automatic	High Compression
SALLHABE3BA000001	2 Door	RH Stg	Automatic	Low Compression
SALLHABE4BA000001	2 Door	LH Stg	Automatic	High Compression
SALLHAMV7BA000001	4 Door	RH Stg	5 Speed	Low Compression
SALLHAMV8BA000001	4 Door	LH Stg	5 Speed	High Compression
SALLHAME7BA000001	4 Door	RH Stg	5 Speed	Low Compression
SALLHAME8BA000001	4 Door	LH Stg	5 Speed	High Compression
SALLHAMV3BA000001	4 Door	RH Stg	Automatic	Low Compression
SALLHAMV4BA000001	4 Door	LH Stg	Automatic	High Compression
SALLHAME3BA000001	4 Door	RH Stg	Automatic	Low Compression
SALLHAME4BA000001	4 Door	LH Stg	Automatic	High Compression

VIN Nos. PETROL RANGE ROVER
86 - On

VIN	Door	Steering	Transmission
SALLHABV7CA000001	2 Door	RH Stg	Manual
SALLHABV8CA000001	2 Door	LH Stg	Manual
SALLHABV3CA000001	2 Door	RH Stg	Automatic
SALLHABV4CA000001	2 Door	LH Stg	Automatic
SALLHAMV7CA000001	4 Door	RH Stg	Manual
SALLHAMV8CA000001	4 Door	LH Stg	Manual
SALLHAMV3CA000001	4 Door	RH Stg	Automatic
SALLHAMV4CA000001	4 Door	LH Stg	Automatic
SALLHAAV7CA000001	2 Door	RH Stg	Manual
SALLHAAV8CA000001	2 Door	LH Stg	Manual
SALLHAAV3CA000001	2 Door	RH Stg	Automatic
SALLHAAV4CA000001	2 Door	LH Stg	Automatic
SALLHABL7CA000001	2 Door	RH Stg	Manual PI
SALLHABL8CA000001	2 Door	LH Stg	Manual PI
SALLHABL3CA000001	2 Door	RH Stg	Automatic PI
SALLHABL4CA000001	2 Door	LH Stg	Automatic PI
SALLHAML7CA000001	4 Door	RH Stg	Manual PI
SALLHAML8CA000001	4 Door	LH Stg	Manual PI
SALLHAML3CA000001	4 Door	RH Stg	Automatic PI
SALLHAML4CA000001	4 Door	LH Stg	Automatic PI

VIN Nos. DIESEL RANGE ROVER
86 - On

VIN	Door	Steering	Transmission
SALLHABE7CA000001	2 Door	RH Stg	204 Manual

SALLHABE8CA000001	2 Door	LH Stg	204 Manual
SALLHAME7CA000001	4 Door	RH Stg	204 Manual
SALLHAME8CA000001	4 Door	LH Stg	204 Manual
SALLHAAE7CA000001	2 Door	RH Stg	204 Manual
SALLHAAE8CA000001	2 Door	LH Stg	204 Manual

Engine Serial Nos

Note B Suffix = Electronic Ignition

35500001C/D/E	8.25:1 C/R — LT 95 Manual gearbox
35500001F	8.13:1 C/R — LT 95 Manual gearbox
34100001C	8.25:1 C/R — Pulsair — Germany, Norway, Sweden — LT 95 Manual gearbox
35900001A	8.25:1 C/R CKD — LT 95 Manual gearbox
39800001F	8.13:1 C/R — Air injection — Australia — LT 95 Manual gearbox
11D00001A	9.35:1 C/R — Pulsair — LT 95 Manual gearbox
13D00001A/B	8.13:1 C/R — Pulsair — Automatic transmission
15300001A/B	9.35:1 C/R — Pulsair — Automatic transmission
16D00001A/B	9.35:1 C/R — Pulsair — Australia — Automatic transmission Evaporation Loss Control
17D00001A/B	9.35:1 C/R — Pulsair — LT 77 Manual gearbox
18D00001A/B	8.13:1 C/R — Pulsair — LT 77 Manual gearbox
19D00001A/B	9.35:1 C/R — Pulsair — Australia LT 77 Manual gearbox
20D00001B	8.13:1 C/R — Pulsair — LT 77 Manual gearbox SAUDI
21D00001B	8.13:1 C/R — Pulsair — Automatic transmission SAUDI
22D00001	8.13:1 C/R — Fuel Injection — Manual gearbox
23D00001	8.13:1 C/R — Fuel Injection — Automatic gearbox
24D00001	9.35:1 C/R — Fuel Injection — Manual gearbox
25D00001	9.35:1 C/R — Fuel Injection — Automatic gearbox
26D00001	9.35:1 C/R — Carburetter detoxed — Manual gearbox
27D00001	9.35:1 C/R — Carburetter detoxed — Automatic gearbox
28D00001	9.35:1 C/R — Carburetter nondetoxed — Manual gearbox
29D00001	9.35:1 C/R — Carburetter nondetoxed — Automatic gearbox
30D00001	8.13:1 C/R — Carburetter detoxed — Manual gearbox

Gearbox Serial Nos

35500001A	LT 95 Manual gearbox, 4 speed
12C00001A	LT 95 Manual gearbox, 4 speed, 1:1 ratio
52A00001A	LT 77 Manual gearbox, 5 speed
PK	Chrysler 727 Automatic transmission
53A00001	LT 77 Manual gearbox, 5 speed
54A00001	LT 77 Manual gearbox, 5 speed, Diesel

Transfer box Serial Nos

14D00001A — LT230R, used with 727 Automatic transmission
15D00001A — LT230R, used with LT77 5 speed manual gearbox
26D00001 — LT230T, used with 727 Automatic transmission
27D00001 — LT230T, used with LT77 5 speed manual gearbox
28D00001 — LT230T, used with LT77 5 speed manual gearbox, V8 and 4 Cylinder Diesel

Axle Serial Nos

35500001A — Front RH Stg
35800001A — Front LH Stg

35500001A — Rear

For your notes

For your notes